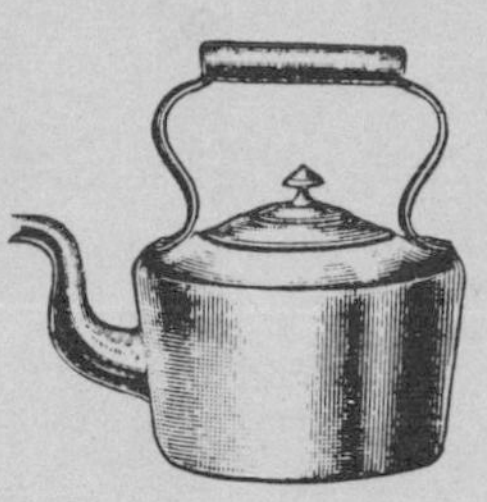

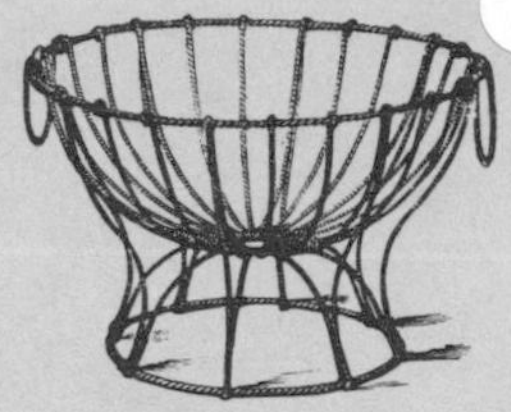

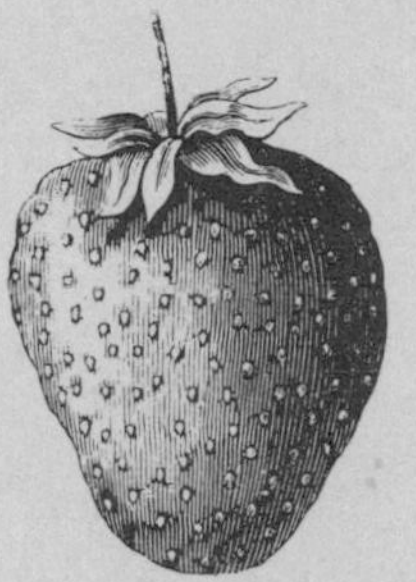

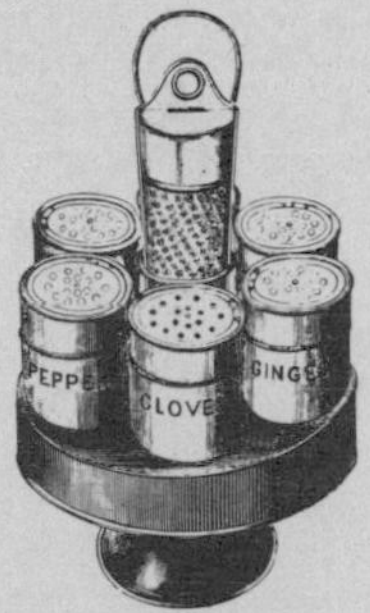

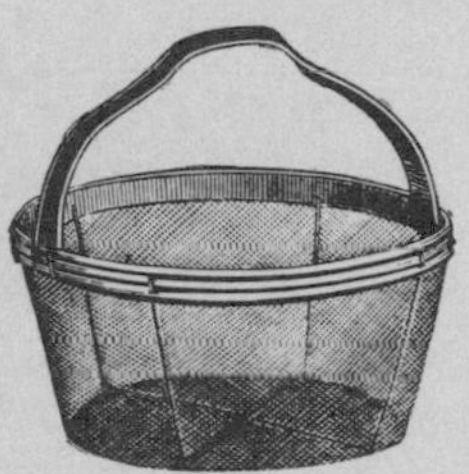

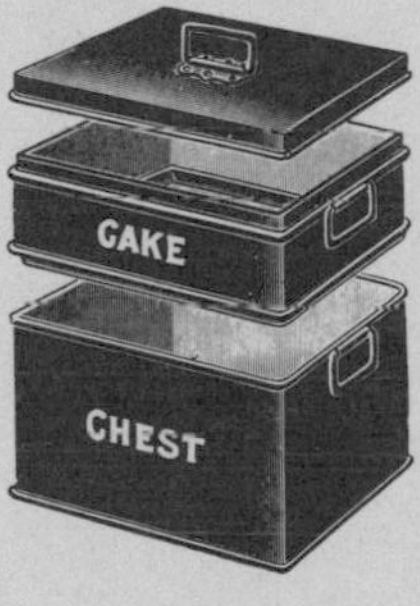
CAKE
CHEST

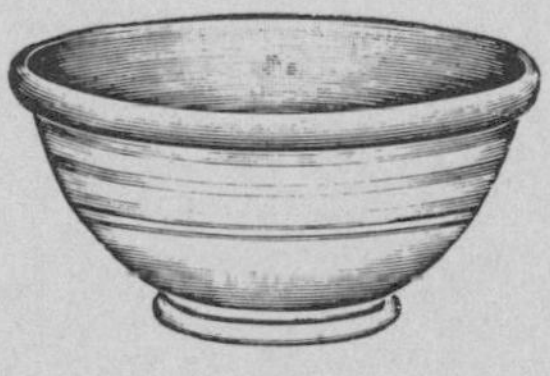

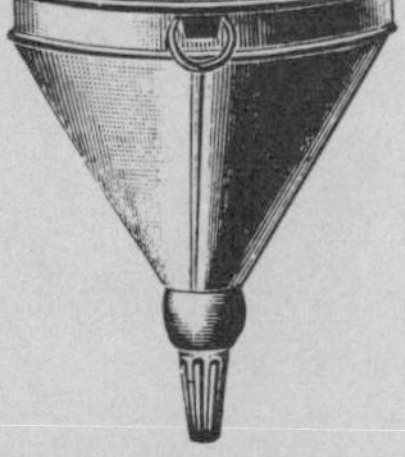

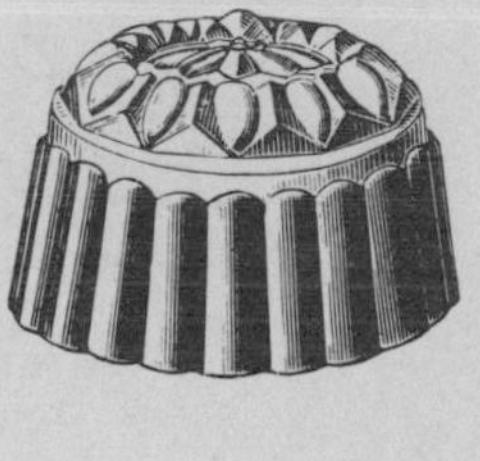

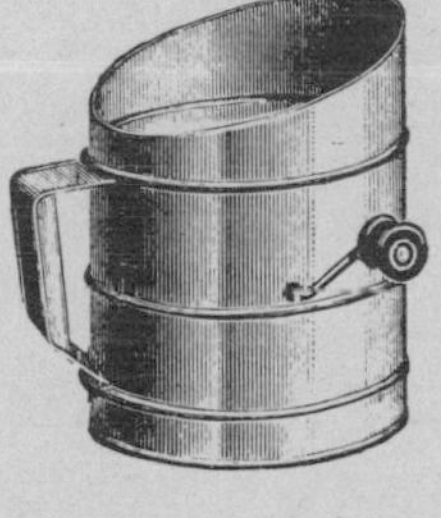

Southern Living.

The SOUTHERN HERITAGE COOKBOOK LIBRARY

The SOUTHERN HERITAGE
Plain and Fancy
Poultry
COOKBOOK

OXMOOR HOUSE
Birmingham, Alabama

Southern Living®

The Southern Heritage Cookbook Library

Library of Congress Catalog Number: 82-62142
ISBN:0-8487-0604-8

Manufactured in the United States of America

The Southern Heritage PLAIN AND FANCY POULTRY Cookbook

Manager, Editorial Projects: Ann H. Harvey
Southern Living® *Foods Editor*: Jean W. Liles
Production Editor: Joan E. Denman
Foods Editor: Katherine M. Eakin
Director, Test Kitchen: Laura N. Nestelroad
Test Kitchen Home Economists: Pattie B. Booker, Kay E. Clarke,
   Nancy Nevins, Elizabeth J. Taliaferro
Production Manager: Jerry R. Higdon
Copy Editor: Melinda E. West
Editorial Assistant: Karen P. Traccarella
Food Photographer: Jim Bathie
Food Stylist: Sara Jane Ball
Layout Designer: Christian von Rosenvinge
Mechanical Artist: Faith Nance
Research Assistant: Janice Randall

Special Consultants

Art Director: Irwin Glusker
Heritage Consultant: Meryle Evans
Foods Writer: Lillian B. Marshall
Food and Recipe Consultants: Marilyn Wyrick Ingram,
   Audrey P. Stehle

Cover (clockwise from back): Roast Turkey (page 31), Roast
Duckling with Orange Sauce (page 43), Country Captain (page 100).
Photograph by Jim Bathie.

CONTENTS

INTRODUCTION

Welcome to the land of Southern Fried! And fricasseed and baked and braised and roasted and stewed with dumplings. Down here in the South, we are crazy about all that fine feathered food, and we've been doing a lot about it since earliest colonial days. We've cooked fowl both wild and domesticated on every sort of heat from campfire to microwave oven and decided we like it. Through the years, breeding has improved the birds we eat, while technology has kept abreast of developments by providing us with food storage and processing equipment that makes child's play of kitchen work.

Chicken has been the fowl most constant in our affections. From man's earliest fires with birds roasting on green sticks to the daintily herbed and sauced "poulet" served in a New Orleans French Quarter restaurant today, we've craved chicken.

Admittedly, chicken has suffered some rejection from snobs through history, but there's no reasoning with some people. For example, at one point during the Middle Ages, chicken became so common in France that royalty scorned it. But the poor, who were in the majority as usual, were happy with the arrangement. They found that the poule-au-pot, a thick soup, provided unfailing and strengthening nourishment.

Then the economy cycled; the poor became poorer, and chickens harder to come by. Royalty rekindled its taste for chicken, taking it effectively out of reach of the general consumer. Henri IV managed to make points with the hungry populace by promising them a chicken every Sunday. When Louisiana Senator Huey P. Long postulated "a chicken in every pot" back in the early 1930s, he was harking back to his history lessons in an effort to marshal the poor to the polls.

Cooks began experimenting with stewing meat as soon as they had fireproof clay pots. The Iron Age laid the foundation for a more substantial kind of cookware, and by the time our East Coast was settled, cooks knew that an iron pot for boiling was the most valuable household item they could own. An iron kettle was a coveted wedding gift. When a cut of meat was too tough for open fire roasting, as it too frequently was, the pot stood ready for stewing.

But when the fowl was tender, everyone adjourned to the outdoors for a barbecue, a spin-off from the original method of spit-roasting, one of the oldest forms of meat cookery. Settlers on the East Coast learned from the Indians to put meats over a green wood fire and sit back while the smoky heat cooked their game to a turn. The Colonials liked the smoked flavor so much that they made it a part of their social life. In the 1700s, New York society took to the outdoor barbecue at the same time politicians discovered it as a rallying point for electioneering. We still turn out in droves at election time, even knowing that a well-tended barbecue pit vies with the political orator in giving off more heat than light.

Many a bride in the early South was given a special gift: a pair of downy geese. Most useful of birds, a goose could live a hundred years. On the way to becoming an heirloom, the goose would lay eggs, hatching some of them under the proper conditions, and provide feathers for all kinds of uses. Not just for feather beds and pillows, mind you, but quills to be sharpened for writing things like letters, novels, and the Declaration of Independence.

When the untimely end came, the goose supplied a feast, with enough excellent grease left over for cooking, for rubbing on the chest of a croupy child, and for polishing boots. For verification and for explicit instructions see the following "recipe" from the 1870s:

Rooster weathervane,
late 1800s

On the day before Christmas, kill a fat goose and dress it. Wash it well in a dishpan of hot soapy water. Rinse in a milk pail of cold water. Dry it thoroughly and hang it in the woodshed over night. Next morning early, mash a kettle of potatoes with cream and butter and a cupful of chopped onion and lots of salt and pepper. Stuff the goose with the potatoes and sew it shut. Rub the skin over with salt and pepper and sage and put it in a not too hot oven. Dip the grease up every hour or so. Note: Keep this grease for use of colds on the chest, or to soften shoes.

Among the native Americans watching the settlers land along the Eastern seaboard were wild turkeys. Europeans had had turkeys since the early explorers brought back specimens in 1518; they recognized them at once. What they were not prepared for was the size and temper of the turkey in the wild. Such a bird could grow as large as fifty pounds. The Pueblos of the Southwest had domesticated the turkey in the sixteenth century, but not for food; their feathers were prized as ornaments and offered as burnt sacrifices.

Despite the admiration of many, there are Southerners among us who still say they don't care for poultry, but mention that by-product, chicken livers, and you may elicit rave responses. Chicken livers, for those who dote on them, can go from a simple omelet to a festive party pâté to a stunning presentation of Chicken Livers Financiére. Enrico Caruso's appetite for pasta was legendary, and just as chicken Tetrazzini was created for the great diva, Spaghetti Caruso was tailored to the man and to two of his favorite foods, pasta and chicken livers. It will be a real find for the chicken liver afficionado. Once you get past the name, Dirty Rice is one of the deep South's main claims to fame...and good eating. Giblets are cooked, ground, and mixed with hot, cooked rice. It is sometimes used as stuffing for fowl or as an accompaniment to an entree, but many a Southerner will tell you that all he needs is a large plate, an unlimited supply of Dirty Rice, and elbow room.

Hen, handcarved from Catalpa wood, mid 1900s

N orth America, to the Europeans, was a cornucopia of good things to eat then as well as now. In the South, they found wild fowl and other small game enough to keep them in meat during the months when it was too warm to bring down large game and risk its spoiling. Hunting is part of the Southerner's background, an avocation that has caused him to take an active part in the enforcement of game laws.

This volume is testimony to the fact that the fowl family is there when we need inspiration. Chapters are based on the various methods used to cook poultry, and introducing each chapter is a menu reflecting a typical way to serve any one of the poultry recipes. Here, then, are some of our best dishes, from plain to fancy.

Female Merganser decoy, early 1900s

OLD TIMERS UP-DATED

In Which We Build Upon Our Past

Fom the day the first fireproof clay pot made stewing possible, man has enjoyed this economical form of cookery. Rather than waste the meat of hens, old and retired from egg laying, and overly matured game and domestic animals often too tough for roasting, frying, or grilling, man discovered that these meats could be made more tender when slow-cooked or stewed in a little liquid. Even if it took all day on a low fire to stew the meat, it was far better than wasting precious meat. Later, the inventive housewife added vegetables, dumplings, and other ingredients to the pot, giving us a legacy of delectable slow-cook dishes—chicken and dumplings, pot-roasted chicken, and that Sunday dinner favorite, chicken fricassee.

For those who may not be familiar with it, fricassee is a sort of chicken and dumplings, without the dumplings.

To refine the definition: A fricassee is the result of a combination of two cooking procedures, frying and stewing. A fricassee contains no vegetables. Those are the rules.

Now for the exceptions: Thomas Jefferson's recipe calls for no frying at all, and it contains mushrooms and onions. Furthermore, his is from the same pool of wisdom as this one from the hand-written cookbook of Eliza Lucas Pinckney of South Carolina, dated 1756:

"To fricassee a chicken White. Flour your chicken and cut it in pieces and put it in a stew pan with some nutmeg, mace and whole pepper, salt, and a little water then thicken it up with gravey, ketchup and white wine, cream and a little flour. You may put in troufles and morels and sweetbreads or oysters. You may do rabbit the same way."

Parenthetically, Eliza Pinckney knew about plenty of things besides cooking. When she was seventeen, her father went on military duty to the West Indies. She not only kept his rice plantation going, but grew the first indigo in this country from seeds her father sent home. Her family was a prestigious one. When she died, President Washington was among the pallbearers.

For a delicious twentieth-century treat, turn the page for our version of Eliza Pinckney's recipe.

Carolina Fricassee Dinner, each ingredient available and popular in the 1700s: Eliza Pinckney's Chicken Fricassee served over hot buttered noodles. Cold Tomato Salad, Summer Squash and Onions, and Whole Steamed Artichokes. Strawberry Shortcake and fresh fruit, a fitting finale.

CAROLINA FRICASSEE DINNER

Brown fricassee came later than the white one. One such variation appeared in *Miss Ann Chase's Book* in 1811. The chicken is coated with seasoned crumbs. Then, "Let the fire be brisk and fry the pieces brown."

"Browning deepens the flavor," cries one faction. "The flavor is much more delicate if you don't brown it," is the rebuttal.

We may, at this point, define fricassee as a preparation, not necessarily of chicken, which may be fried brown or light or not at all. It may contain onions, "troufles," oysters, or none of the above. Whatever it is, let's leave off defining it and make a fricassee. In the menu, we'll include another Colonial favorite, "Harty Choaks." Artichokes were popular and cheap enough in those days that only the bottoms were used, never the leaves.

WHOLE STEAMED ARTICHOKES
ELIZA PINCKNEY'S CHICKEN FRICASSEE
SUMMER SQUASH AND ONIONS
COLD TOMATO SALAD
STRAWBERRY SHORTCAKE

Serves 4 to 6

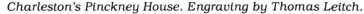

WHOLE STEAMED ARTICHOKES

6 artichokes
Lemon wedge
Clarified Butter Sauce

Wash artichokes by plunging up and down in cold water. Cut off the stem end, and trim about ½ inch from top of each artichoke. Remove any loose bottom leaves. With scissors, trim away one-fourth of each outer leaf. Rub top and edges of leaves of each artichoke with a lemon wedge to prevent discoloration.

Place artichokes in a large Dutch oven with about 1 inch of water. Bring to a boil; cover and reduce heat. Simmer 40 to 45 minutes or until leaves pull out easily. Spread leaves apart; remove fuzzy thistle center (choke) with a spoon.

Arrange the artichokes on individual serving plates, and serve with Clarified Butter Sauce. Yield: 6 servings.

Clarified Butter Sauce:

1 cup butter
1 tablespoon plus 1 teaspoon Dijon mustard
Juice of 1 lemon

Melt butter over low heat in a 1-quart saucepan. The fat will rise to the top, and the milk solids will sink to the bottom. Remove from heat. Skim the white froth off the top. Strain off the clear yellow butter, keeping back the sediment of milk solids. Discard the milk solids. Combine the clarified butter, mustard, and lemon juice, mixing well. Yield: about 1 cup.

Charleston's Pinckney House. Engraving by Thomas Leitch.

ELIZA PINCKNEY'S CHICKEN FRICASSEE

½ cup all-purpose flour
1 teaspoon salt
½ teaspoon pepper
¼ teaspoon ground mace
¼ teaspoon ground
   nutmeg
1 (3- to 4-pound) broiler-fryer,
   cut up
⅓ cup vegetable oil
1 large onion, sliced
1 (2½-ounce) jar mushroom
   caps, drained
2 chicken-flavored bouillon
   cubes
3 cups boiling water
2 tablespoons catsup
¼ cup commercial sour
   cream
¼ cup Chablis or other dry
   white wine
1 teaspoon prepared
   mustard
Hot cooked noodles
Chopped fresh parsley
   (optional)

Combine flour, salt, pepper, mace, and nutmeg in a bowl; mix well. Dredge chicken in flour mixture.

Heat oil in a large skillet to 325°. Add dredged chicken, and fry 10 to 15 minutes or until golden brown, turning occasionally.

Place onion and mushrooms over chicken; cook 5 minutes or until onion and mushrooms are tender. Dissolve bouillon cubes in boiling water; pour over chicken. Cover and simmer over low heat 3 hours or until chicken is tender. Skim off excess fat.

Combine catsup, sour cream, wine, and mustard in a small bowl; mix well. Spoon mixture over chicken in skillet, and heat thoroughly. Serve chicken on a bed of hot cooked noodles. Sprinkle with chopped parsley, if desired. Yield: 4 to 6 servings.

Note: If slow cooker is used, brown chicken in a skillet before placing in slow cooker. Cook on low for 7 to 8 hours or on high for 4 to 5 hours. Add sauce mixture during last 30 minutes of cooking time.

SUMMER SQUASH AND ONIONS

3 tablespoons bacon
   drippings
3 small onions, chopped
2 pounds yellow squash, cut
   into ¼-inch thick slices
½ cup water
½ teaspoon salt
¼ teaspoon pepper

Heat bacon drippings in a skillet over medium heat. Add onion, and sauté until tender but not brown. Add squash, water, salt, and pepper. Reduce heat; cover and simmer 20 minutes or until squash is tender. Yield: 6 servings.

COLD TOMATO SALAD

2 tablespoons vegetable oil
1 tablespoon vinegar
½ teaspoon salt
¼ teaspoon pepper
4 medium tomatoes, sliced

Combine first 4 ingredients in a jar; shake well. Pour marinade over tomatoes; refrigerate 2 hours before serving. Yield: 4 to 6 servings.

STRAWBERRY SHORTCAKE

2 cups all-purpose flour
½ cup sugar, divided
1 teaspoon baking soda
½ teaspoon salt
⅓ cup butter
1 cup buttermilk
1 egg
½ cup butter, softened
1 cup whipping cream
1 pint strawberries, sliced
¼ cup plus 2 tablespoons
   sifted powdered sugar
Whole strawberries

Combine flour, ¼ cup sugar, soda, and salt in a large mixing bowl; cut in ⅓ cup butter with a pastry blender until mixture resembles coarse meal.

Combine buttermilk and egg, beating well. Add to flour mixture; stir with a fork until a soft dough forms. Pat half of dough into a well-greased 9-inch round cakepan. (Dough will be sticky; dust hands with flour.)

Spread ½ cup butter evenly over dough in pan; pat remaining dough evenly over butter layer. Bake at 425° for 20 minutes or until golden brown. Remove from pan while still warm; split the 2 layers.

Beat whipping cream until foamy; gradually add remaining ¼ cup sugar, beating until soft peaks form.

Place 1 cake layer on serving plate. Arrange sliced strawberries on top of cake layer. Sprinkle with ¼ cup powdered sugar. Cover with remaining cake layer, and sprinkle remaining 2 tablespoons powdered sugar over top. Garnish shortcake with whole strawberries. Serve with sweetened whipped cream. Yield: 8 to 10 servings.

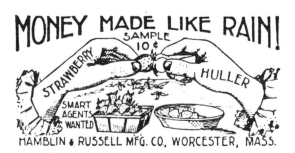

FRICASSEES

A BROWN FRICASSEE

2 cups soft breadcrumbs
1 teaspoon salt
½ teaspoon pepper
½ teaspoon ground
   nutmeg
½ teaspoon ground mace
1 (3½- to 4-pound)
   broiler-fryer, cut up
2 egg yolks, beaten
½ cup butter or margarine
2 cups chicken broth
1 cup red wine
½ cup sliced fresh
   mushrooms
2 tablespoons all-purpose
   flour
Hot mashed potatoes

Combine first 5 ingredients, and stir well.

Rinse chicken with cold water, and pat dry. Dip chicken in egg yolks, and dredge in breadcrumb mixture.

Melt butter in a large skillet. Add chicken, and cook over medium heat 10 minutes, turning to brown all sides. Add chicken broth, wine, and mushrooms; cover and simmer 30 minutes.

Blend flour with a small amount of water, mixing to form a smooth paste; stir into chicken mixture. Cook until thickened and bubbly. Serve over hot mashed potatoes. Yield: 4 to 6 servings.

Poultry Journal, c.1900.

Stew-Hole chicken fricassee prepared the traditional way.

In the seventeenth century, there came into existence a sophisticated masonry counter-top unit that was a forerunner of our present-day stove top. In New Orleans, where it was widely used, it was called a stew-hole. The eighteenth-century French term for it was potager; the English called it a stewing hearth. It is still used in parts of Mexico and Central America.

An auxiliary to the open fireplace, the stew-hole was made for slow, even cooking. There were holes in the counter where pots could be placed over an iron grid. Under each hole was a compartment to hold hot coals, and at the base was a log fireplace in which one could prepare the coals for these compartments.

One of the most singular attractions at the historic Hermann-Grima House in New Orleans today is the working kitchen where demonstrations are given, using the original equipment, including the stew-hole. Now owned by the Christian Women's Exchange, the handsome Hermann-Grima House is open to the public, helping visitors to appreciate what a feat it was to produce a meal even in the best-equipped 1831 kitchen. The kitchens of great houses were traditionally built separately from the main house because of the omnipresent hazard of fire, and grease fires were most destructive of all. The stew-hole gave the skillet and frying a secure place in Southern cuisine.

STEW-HOLE CHICKEN FRICASSEE

1 (3-pound) broiler-fryer,
  cut up
½ cup bacon drippings
1 large onion, chopped
4 stalks celery, chopped
1 large green pepper,
  chopped
½ cup all-purpose flour
2 cups chicken broth
3 bay leaves
1 large tomato, peeled,
  seeded, and chopped
½ teaspoon salt
¼ teaspoon pepper
8 to 10 drops hot sauce
Hot cooked rice

Brown chicken in hot bacon drippings in a Dutch oven. Remove chicken from Dutch oven, and drain on paper towels.

Add onion, celery, and green pepper to hot bacon drippings; cook until tender. Place flour in a small skillet; cook over medium heat, stirring constantly, until golden brown. Gradually add browned flour to sautéed vegetables, stirring constantly. Cook 1 minute over medium heat. Gradually add broth; stir well. Stir in next 5 ingredients. Return chicken to Dutch oven; cover and cook over low heat for 1 hour. Remove lid, and cook an additional hour. Remove bay leaves. Serve over hot cooked rice. Yield: 4 to 6 servings.

MARION HARLAND'S FRICASSEE

¼ pound salt pork, cut
  into strips
1 small onion, sliced
1½ cups water
1 (3- to 3½-pound)
  broiler-fryer, cut up and
  skinned
½ teaspoon salt
½ to ¾ teaspoon ground
  allspice
½ to ¾ teaspooon ground
  cloves
¾ cup all-purpose
  flour
½ cup dry sherry
1 tablespoon catsup
1 teaspoon chopped fresh
  parsley
Hot cooked rice (optional)

Cook salt pork in a small skillet until crisp; drain on paper towels. Chop finely and set aside, reserving drippings in skillet.

Sauté onion in drippings 3 to 5 minutes. Combine salt pork, onion, water, chicken, salt, allspice, and cloves in a Dutch oven. Cover and simmer 30 minutes or until chicken is tender. Remove chicken from juices, and keep warm.

Place flour in a small skillet; cook over medium heat, stirring frequently, until browned. Stir in sherry, catsup, and parsley; add to pan juices, stirring until smooth. Cook over medium heat, stirring constantly, until thickened and bubbly. Strain gravy to remove salt pork and onions.

Return chicken and gravy to Dutch oven, and heat thoroughly. Serve over hot cooked rice, if desired. Yield: 4 servings.

A WHITE FRICASSEE

1 (3- to 3½-pound)
  broiler-fryer, cut up
1 cup milk
1 cup water
1 teaspoon salt
½ teaspoon pepper
¼ cup butter or margarine
¼ cup all-purpose flour
¼ teaspoon ground mace
¼ teaspoon pepper
1 cup whipping cream
Hot cooked rice

Rinse chicken with cold water, and place in a large Dutch oven. Add milk, water, salt, and ½ teaspoon pepper; simmer over low heat 30 minutes. Remove chicken from broth, reserving 1 cup broth. Remove skin from chicken, and set aside.

Melt butter over low heat; add flour, mace, and ¼ teaspoon pepper. Stir until smooth. Cook 1 minute, stirring constantly. Gradually add reserved broth and whipping cream; cook over medium heat, stirring constantly, until thickened and bubbly. Serve chicken on a bed of rice. Spoon white sauce over chicken. Yield: 4 to 6 servings.

THOMAS JEFFERSON'S FRICASSEE

1 teaspoon dried whole
  thyme
½ teaspoon whole
  peppercorns
2 sprigs fresh parsley
1 bay leaf
3 cups boiling water
2 (3- to 4-pound)
  broiler-fryers, cut up and
  skinned
1 teaspoon salt
¼ teaspoon pepper
3 tablespoons water
1½ tablespoons all-purpose
  flour
16 small fresh mushrooms
6 small onions
2 egg yolks
1 tablespoon lemon juice

Combine thyme, peppercorns, parsley, and bay leaf in a cheesecloth bag. Combine boiling water, chicken, herb bag, salt, and pepper in a large Dutch oven. Cover and let stand 10 minutes. Remove chicken and herb bag; set aside. Strain liquid; set aside.

Add 3 tablespoons water to Dutch oven; gradually add flour, stirring to blend thoroughly. Add chicken, herb bag, and reserved liquid. Cover and simmer for 30 minutes. Add mushrooms and onions to chicken mixture. Cover and simmer an additional 30 minutes.

Remove chicken to a serving platter; keep warm. Discard herb bag.

Combine yolks and lemon juice. Gradually stir a small amount of hot broth mixture into yolk mixture; add to remaining hot mixture, stirring constantly. Cook over low heat 2 minutes or until thickened. Pour sauce over chicken. Yield: 8 servings.

WHITE WINE FRICASSEE

1 (3- to 3½-pound)
  broiler-fryer, cut up and
  skinned
⅓ cup milk
⅓ cup water
½ cup milk
½ cup whipping cream
¼ cup Chablis or other dry
  white wine
2 tablespoons butter or
  margarine
3 tablespoons all-purpose
  flour
½ teaspoon salt
¼ teaspoon ground
  nutmeg
Pinch of ground mace

Place chicken in a Dutch oven; add ⅓ cup milk and water and bring to a boil. Reduce heat; cover and simmer 40 minutes or until chicken is tender. Remove chicken from Dutch oven, draining off broth. Transfer chicken to a serving platter.

Combine ½ cup milk, whipping cream, and wine; set aside. Melt butter in a heavy saucepan over low heat; add flour, stirring until smooth. Cook 1 minute, stirring constantly. Gradually add milk mixture; cook over medium heat, stirring constantly, until thickened and bubbly. Add remaining ingredients; blend well. Spoon sauce over chicken. Yield: 4 servings.

Handwritten recipe for Fricassee Chicken from the manuscript for Recipes in the Culinary Art, *1852.*

Civilised Poultry.

Fricasee Chickens

The chickens are put on in a little water, and a slice of bacon and some salt to season it. Then beat up the eggs (an egg to a chicken) with a little flour, dip up some of the hot liquor from the chickens and stir in first; then pour in the egg and it is soon done, then put in the butter and bread.

FOUNDATION COOKING

OLD-FASHIONED SIMMERED CHICKEN

1 (3- to 3½-pound) broiler-fryer
2 stalks celery with leaves, halved
1 medium onion
3 sprigs fresh parsley
1 teaspoon salt
1 bay leaf
½ teaspoon dried whole rosemary
¼ teaspoon whole peppercorns
6 cups water
Hot cooked rice

Combine all ingredients except rice in a large Dutch oven; bring to a boil. Cover mixture; reduce heat, and simmer 40 minutes or until chicken is tender. Remove chicken from broth; cool. Bone chicken, and serve with hot cooked rice. Reserve chicken broth for other uses. Yield: 4 servings.

Note: Chicken may be cut into bite-size pieces for use in other recipes.

BOILED CHICKEN WITH BUTTER SAUCE

1 (3-pound) broiler-fryer, cut up
1 tablespoon salt
¼ teaspoon pepper
¼ cup plus 2 tablespoons butter, melted
½ cup plus 1 tablespoon lemon juice
3 tablespoons chopped fresh parsley

Sprinkle chicken with salt and pepper; place in a Dutch oven, and cover with water. Bring to a boil. Cover; reduce heat, and simmer 1 hour or until chicken is tender. Remove to serving platter.

Combine butter, lemon juice, and parsley; stir until well blended. Serve with chicken. Yield: 4 servings.

Shake hands? *Lithograph after Lilly Spencer's painting, 1854.*

STEWED CHICKEN WITH BISCUITS

1 (3-pound) broiler-fryer, cut up and skinned
8 hot biscuits, halved
3 tablespoons butter or margarine, melted
¼ cup all-purpose flour
¼ teaspoon salt
⅛ teaspoon pepper
Pimiento strips (optional)

Place chicken in a Dutch oven, and cover with water; bring to a boil. Cover; reduce heat, and simmer 2 hours or until chicken is tender. Remove chicken from broth; cool. Bone chicken, and cut into bite-size pieces. Arrange chicken over each biscuit half; keep warm.

Reduce broth to 1½ cups by boiling over high heat. Combine butter and flour, stirring well to make a smooth paste. Gradually add to boiling broth, stirring constantly. Reduce heat, and add salt and pepper. Cook over medium heat, stirring constantly, until thickened and bubbly. Pour gravy over chicken and biscuits. Garnish with pimiento strips, if desired. Yield: 8 servings.

CAROLINA CHICKEN AND DROP DUMPLINGS

1 (4-pound) stewing hen,
  cut up
2 cups all-purpose flour
1 tablespoon baking
  powder
1 teaspoon salt
2 tablespoons butter or
  margarine
1 cup milk
3 tablespoons all-purpose
  flour
1 cup milk
½ teaspoon salt
¼ teaspoon pepper

Place chicken in a large Dutch oven, and cover with water; bring to a boil. Cover, reduce heat, and simmer 2 hours. Uncover, and simmer an additional 30 minutes or until chicken is tender and broth is reduced by half. Remove chicken from broth; cool. Bone chicken, and cut into bite-size pieces. Set chicken and broth aside.

Combine next 3 ingredients; cut in butter with pastry blender until mixture resembles coarse meal. Add 1 cup milk; stir until well blended. Bring reserved broth to a boil. Drop batter by heaping tablespoonfuls into boiling broth, allowing room for dumplings to expand during cooking process. Cover immediately; reduce heat, and simmer 12 minutes or until a wooden pick inserted in center of each dumpling comes out clean. Repeat procedure with remaining batter, if necessary. Transfer chicken and dumplings to serving platter, and keep warm.

Cook remaining broth over high heat until reduced by half. Add 3 tablespoons flour to broth, stirring until smooth. Cook 3 minutes, stirring constantly. Gradually add 1 cup milk, stirring well. Cook over medium heat, stirring constantly, until thickened. Stir in ½ teaspoon salt and pepper. Pour gravy over chicken and dumplings. Yield: 6 servings.

Note: Dumplings are primarily cooked by steam heat, and should be kept covered during cooking. To prevent overcrowding of dumplings, allow room for expansion when placing batter in broth.

CHICKEN AND DROP DUMPLINGS, TEXAS-STYLE

1 (5-pound) baking hen,
  cut up
2 quarts water
¼ cup chopped fresh celery
  leaves
2½ teaspoons salt, divided
½ teaspoon pepper, divided
2½ cups all-purpose flour,
  divided
1 cup cold water
3 tablespoons shortening
1 egg, beaten
¾ cup milk

Combine first 3 ingredients with 2 teaspoons salt, and ¼ teaspoon pepper in a large Dutch oven. Bring to a boil. Cover, reduce heat, and simmer 2½ hours or until chicken is tender. Remove chicken from broth; cool. Bone chicken, and cut into bite-size pieces; set aside. Strain broth.

Combine ½ cup flour and 1 cup water, blending well; add to broth in Dutch oven, stirring until smooth. Stir in chicken.

Combine remaining flour, salt, and pepper; stir well. Cut in shortening with a pastry blender until mixture resembles coarse meal. Stir in egg and milk. Bring broth mixture to a boil. Drop dumpling batter by tablespoonfuls into broth mixture, allowing room for expansion. Cover; reduce heat and simmer 15 minutes or until a wooden pick inserted in center comes out clean. Repeat procedure with remaining batter. Yield: 6 servings.

STEWED CHICKEN WITH LIGHT DUMPLINGS

1 (5½- to 6-pound) baking
  hen, cut up
3 to 4 fresh celery leaves
1 medium onion, chopped
1 bay leaf
Pinch of ground thyme
1 tablespoon salt
¼ teaspoon pepper
¼ cup plus 1 tablespoon
  all-purpose flour
2 tablespoons butter or
  margarine, melted
1 cup all-purpose flour
1 teaspoon baking powder
Pinch of baking soda
1 tablespoon butter or
  margarine, melted
½ cup milk

Combine first 7 ingredients in a Dutch oven, and cover with water; bring to a boil. Cover; reduce heat, and simmer 4 hours or until chicken is tender. Remove chicken from broth; cool. Bone chicken, and cut into bite-size pieces. Set aside. Strain broth, and set aside.

Combine ¼ cup plus 1 tablespoon flour and 2 tablespoons melted butter; stir well to make a paste. Gradually add paste to broth, stirring until smooth. Cook over medium heat, stirring constantly, until thickened and bubbly. Stir in chicken.

Combine 1 cup flour, baking powder, baking soda, 1 tablespoon butter, and milk; stir well. Drop batter by tablespoonfuls into boiling broth mixture, allowing room for dumplings to expand during cooking process. Cover immediately; reduce heat, and simmer 20 minutes or until a wooden pick inserted in center of each dumpling comes out clean. Repeat procedure with remaining batter, if necessary. Serve immediately. Yield: 6 to 8 servings.

With Light Dumplings (front) or "Slipperies" (rear): Chicken!

CHICKEN AND SLIPPERY DUMPLINGS

1 (3- to 4-pound) broiler-fryer
1 large onion, halved
1 large carrot, halved
1 stalk celery with leaves, halved
1½ teaspoons salt
½ teaspoon pepper
2 quarts water
2 cups all-purpose flour
1 teaspoon salt
2 tablespoons shortening
½ cup hot water
⅓ cup all-purpose flour

Combine first 7 ingredients in a large Dutch oven; bring to a boil. Cover, reduce heat, and simmer 1 hour or until chicken is tender. Remove chicken from broth; cool. Strain broth. Bone chicken, and cut into bite-size pieces. Return chicken to broth; set aside.

Combine 2 cups flour and 1 teaspoon salt; cut in shortening with a pastry blender until mixture resembles coarse meal. Stir in hot water with a fork until dry ingredients are moistened. Turn dough out onto a lightly floured surface. Roll dough to 1/16-inch thickness; cut into 1- x 3-inch strips. Bring chicken broth to a boil. Drop dumpling strips into broth. Cover; reduce heat, and simmer 20 minutes or until dumplings are plump and tender. Transfer chicken and dumplings to a serving platter.

Blend ⅓ cup flour with a small amount of water, mixing to form a smooth paste; add to broth, stirring until smooth. Cook, stirring constantly, until thickened and bubbly. Pour over chicken and dumplings. Yield: 4 to 6 servings.

Southerners have strong preferences about their dumplings. Before baking powder, dumplings had more of a chewy, noodle-like consistency than the fluffy ones many of us make today, and they still have their partisans. Rolled out and cut into strips or dropped from a spoon, each dumpling should land in a different spot. Down the Eastern shore, they make "slick" or "slippery" dumplings without baking powder; nothing's more delicious. Unless your heritage is German. Ah, potato dumplings!

SATURDAY

Nineteenth-century advertising card: Rolling dumplings.

CHICKEN AND SLICK DUMPLINGS

1 (5-pound) baking hen
2 quarts water
1 teaspoon salt
¼ cup shortening
2 cups self-rising flour
¾ cup boiling water
Salt and pepper to taste

Combine chicken, 2 quarts water, and 1 teaspoon salt in a large Dutch oven; bring to a boil. Reduce heat, cover, and simmer 2½ hours or until chicken is tender. If necessary, add water to maintain at least 3 cups broth. Remove chicken from broth; cool. Bone chicken, and cut into bite-size pieces. Return chicken pieces to broth, and set aside.

Cut shortening into flour with a pastry blender until mixture resembles coarse meal. Add boiling water, stirring with a fork until dry ingredients are moistened. Turn dough out onto a lightly floured surface; roll to ⅛-inch thickness, and cut into ½-x 3-inch strips.

Bring broth to a boil. Drop dumplings into broth. Cover immediately; reduce heat, and simmer 10 minutes. Add salt and pepper to taste. Serve immediately. Yield: 6 servings.

CHICKEN AND ROLLED DUMPLINGS

1 (5- to 6-pound) baking hen
2 teaspoons salt, divided
1 cup all-purpose flour
1 teaspoon baking powder
3 tablespoons shortening
¼ cup milk

Place chicken and 1½ teaspoons salt in a small Dutch oven, cover with water, and bring to a boil. Cover, reduce heat, and simmer 3½ hours or until chicken is tender. If necessary, add water to maintain at least 3 cups broth. Remove chicken from broth; cool. Bone chicken, and cut into bite-size pieces. Return chicken to broth, and set aside.

Combine flour, baking powder, and remaining salt, stirring well. Cut in shortening with a pastry blender until mixture resembles coarse meal. Add milk, stirring to form a soft dough. Turn out onto a lightly floured surface, and knead gently 30 seconds. Roll dough to ⅛-inch thickness; cut into 2-inch squares. Bring chicken broth to a boil. Drop dumpling squares into broth. Cover; reduce heat, and simmer 10 minutes or until dumplings are plump and tender. Yield: 6 to 8 servings.

Note: The dough must be rolled very thin to create a good rolled dumpling.

O n the surface, it might appear that there is little difference between the processes of boiling and stewing. However, boiling is used very little except to originate the stewing process, to reduce liquid after the meat has been removed, and for a few foods such as pasta which require a full rolling boil. Among the most valuable utensils the colonists brought to the New World were their iron kettles. These were hung over the open fire by hooks of varying heights to regulate the distance between the pot and the fire.

The iron pot simmered over to the side after the boil had been reached; in those days, one simply started early and allowed nature to take its course. By and by the chicken would be tender; there was no way to rush matters. With a succulent bird in the pot surrounded by nourishing broth, the next logical step was to extend the meal by adding good things to the liquid. Now the cook was in a position to make chicken and dumplings or the richest of soups.

CHICKEN AND PLUMP DUMPLINGS

1 (2½- to 3-pound) broiler-fryer, cut up and skinned
1 teaspoon chicken-flavored bouillon granules
1 tablespoon salt
¼ teaspoon pepper
2 cups all-purpose flour
1 teaspoon baking powder
1 teaspoon salt
⅛ teaspoon pepper
⅓ cup lard
½ cup milk

Combine chicken, bouillon, 1 tablespoon salt, and ¼ teaspoon pepper in a Dutch oven. Cover with water, and bring to a boil. Cover, reduce heat, and simmer 1½ hours or until chicken is tender. Remove chicken from broth; cool. Bone chicken, and cut into bite-size pieces. Return chicken to broth; set aside.

Combine flour, baking powder, 1 teaspoon salt, and ⅛ teaspoon pepper, mixing well. Cut lard into flour mixture with a pastry blender until mixture resembles coarse meal. Add milk, stirring with a fork until dry ingredients are moistened. Turn dough out onto a lightly floured surface; knead gently 30 seconds. Roll dough to ⅛-inch thickness; cut into 1- x 4-inch strips. Bring chicken broth to a boil. Drop dumpling strips into broth. Reduce heat; cook, uncovered, 20 minutes. Cover, and continue cooking 5 minutes or until dumplings are plump and tender. Yield: 6 to 8 servings.

Note: The addition of chicken-flavored bouillon granules is a "modern" innovation that serves to make the chicken broth "headier."

POTATO DUMPLINGS

2 large potatoes, peeled and grated
1 cup all-purpose flour
½ teaspoon baking powder
¼ teaspoon salt
¼ teaspoon white pepper
1 egg, beaten
1 tablespoon butter or margarine, melted
About 6 cups chicken broth

Squeeze all excess liquid from grated potatoes. Combine potatoes and next 4 ingredients, stirring well. Add egg and butter; mix until well blended. Shape into 1½-inch balls. Drop dumplings into boiling broth. Cover; reduce heat, and simmer 25 minutes or until a wooden pick inserted in center of dumpling comes out clean. Yield: 4 to 6 servings.

Note: These are delicious alone or may accompany any stewed dish.

Poultryman at right appears to thrive on Sheridan's too.

"Modern" nineteenth-century range accommodated varied cooking activities.

CHICKEN NOODLE SOUP

2 tablespoons milk
2 eggs
About 1⅓ cups all-purpose
   flour
1 (3- to 3½-pound)
   broiler-fryer, cut up
3 tablespoons uncooked
   regular rice
1 medium onion
1 teaspoon salt
½ teaspoon pepper

Combine milk and eggs, beating well. Gradually stir in flour until mixture forms a soft dough. Divide the dough into three equal portions. Roll each portion to 1/16-inch thickness on a lightly floured surface; cut into ½- x 4-inch strips. Let stand on floured surface at room temperature 2 hours or until dry.

Combine chicken, rice, onion, salt, and pepper in a large Dutch oven. Add water to cover and bring to a boil. Cover; reduce heat, and simmer 1 hour or until chicken is tender. Remove onion from broth, and discard. Remove chicken from broth; bone, and chop chicken. Return chicken to broth, and bring to a boil.

Drop dried noodles into boiling broth; cook, uncovered, 30 minutes or until noodles are tender. Yield: about 8 cups.

HEARTY CHICKEN SOUP

3 medium onions, chopped
6 stalks celery, chopped
½ cup butter or margarine
1 tablespoon all-purpose
   flour
1 (3- to 3½-pound)
   broiler-fryer, cut up and
   skinned
8 cups water
1½ teaspoons whole
   peppercorns
1½ teaspoons salt
1 cup whipping cream
¼ cup plus 2 tablespoons
   all-purpose flour
Hot cooked rice

Sauté onions and celery in butter in a large Dutch oven until tender. Sprinkle 1 tablespoon flour over sautéed vegetables; stir well. Cook over low heat 10 minutes, stirring occasionally.

Add chicken, water, peppercorns, and salt to Dutch oven; bring to a boil. Cover; reduce heat, and simmer 1 hour or until chicken is tender.

Remove chicken from broth; bone, and chop chicken. Strain broth, and discard vegetables. Skim off excess fat. Return chicken and broth to Dutch oven. Combine whipping cream and ¼ cup plus 2 tablespoons flour; stir into broth. Cook over medium heat, stirring constantly, until mixture is thick and bubbly. Serve immediately over rice. Yield: 6 cups.

BRAISED AND SMOTHERED

POT-ROASTED CHICKEN

1 (4½- to 5-pound)
  baking hen
¼ cup butter or margarine
1 cup Chablis or other dry
  white wine
1 cup chicken broth
2 teaspoons salt
12 new potatoes, unpeeled
18 baby carrots
18 pearl onions
12 fresh mushrooms, halved
½ cup chopped fresh celery
  leaves
¼ teaspoon dried whole
  rosemary
¼ cup all-purpose flour

Remove giblets from cavity of chicken, and reserve for other uses. Rinse chicken with cold water, and pat dry. Tie ends of legs to tail with string. Lift wingtips up and over back so they are tucked under chicken securely.

Melt butter in a large skillet. Brown chicken in butter over low heat; transfer to a large Dutch oven, reserving butter in skillet.

Combine wine, broth, and salt; pour into skillet, and stir well. Bring mixture to a boil. Remove from heat, and pour over chicken. Cover and cook over medium heat 45 minutes.

Cut the cord holding the drumstick ends to the tail; this will ensure that the inside of the thighs are cooked. Layer potatoes, carrots, onions, mushrooms, celery leaves, and rosemary around chicken in Dutch oven. Cover and cook over medium heat an additional hour or until drumsticks are easy to move. Remove chicken and vegetables to serving platter, and keep warm.

Bring pan drippings to a boil; gradually add flour, stirring constantly, until thickened and bubbly. Serve gravy with chicken and vegetables. Yield: 6 to 8 servings.

TEXAS BRAISED CHICKEN

1 cup finely crushed cracker
  crumbs
1 teaspoon salt
½ teaspoon pepper
1 (3- to 3½-pound)
  broiler-fryer, cut up
1 egg, beaten
¼ cup butter or margarine
¼ cup lard
1 cup water
2 medium tomatoes, chopped
2 tablespoons chopped
  green pepper
3 cups hot cooked rice
Fresh parsley sprigs

Combine first 3 ingredients, stirring well. Set aside.

Rinse chicken with cold water, and pat dry. Dip chicken in egg, and dredge in cracker crumb mixture.

Melt butter and lard in a large skillet. Add chicken, and cook over medium heat 10 minutes, turning to brown on all sides. Add water; cover and simmer 30 minutes. Remove chicken from skillet, and keep warm. Reserve pan drippings.

Add tomatoes and green pepper to pan drippings; cook over medium heat 3 minutes. Stir in rice, and mix well. Spoon rice mixture in center of a serving platter; arrange chicken pieces on rice. Garnish with parsley. Yield: 4 to 6 servings.

Getting further into moist cookery, we come to smothering and braising. Smothering is a simple term used for cooking anything in liquid in a covered container. It can be applied to duck or rabbit, or even parsnips, as well as to poultry. Smothering implies more liquid than is used in braising. Evaporation is kept to a minimum, the flavor stays in the pot, and that liquid may be thickened for a gravy to serve over or around the finished dish. Southerners have been known to use rice for making the most of their gravy. Braising is so-called for the brazier, a heavy pot with a tight-fitting lid. A "braise" technically consists of some chopped vegetables and other flavorings plus a little liquid. To braise meat, then, is to cook it with flavor additives in a tightly covered  pot. The food is sometimes browned before braising. The braised vegetables are occasionally discarded, and the strained liquid served as is or thickened with flour for gravy. A large, potentially tough bird may be pot-roasted like an economy cut of beef as in the recipe above. For a pot-roasted hen, the vegetables are added after the chicken has cooked almost tender. But whether the braising or pot-roasting method is used, long, moist cooking is required.

Virginia Smothered Chicken (left) has been cooked over the years in fireplaces, stew-holes, and perhaps in the oven of "Peninsular Brand" ranges.

VIRGINIA SMOTHERED CHICKEN

¾ cup all-purpose flour, divided
2 teaspoons salt
1 teaspoon pepper
2 (2½- to 3-pound) broiler-fryers, split
1 cup butter or margarine, melted
2 cups boiling water
⅔ cup water
1½ tablespoons lemon juice
Hot cooked rice

Combine ½ cup flour, salt, and pepper in a bowl; mix well. Dredge chicken in flour mixture. Place chicken in a 5-quart casserole; pour melted butter and boiling water over chicken. Cover and bake at 350° for 1½ hours. Remove cover, and continue baking 15 minutes or until chicken is brown, basting occasionally with pan drippings. Remove chicken; set aside, and keep warm. Reserve ¼ cup pan drippings.

Combine remaining flour and reserved pan drippings in a skillet, stirring until smooth. Cook 1 minute over medium heat, stirring constantly. Gradually add ⅔ cup water, stirring well; cook, stirring constantly, until thickened and bubbly. Stir in lemon juice. Place chicken on a bed of rice on a serving platter, and pour gravy over top. Yield: 6 to 8 servings.

SMOTHERED CHICKEN AND GRAVY

½ cup all-purpose flour
½ teaspoon salt
½ teaspoon pepper
1 (2- to 2½-pound) broiler-fryer, cut up
¼ cup butter or margarine, melted
1 cup half-and-half, divided
1 tablespoon all-purpose flour
Salt and pepper to taste

Combine ½ cup flour, ½ teaspoon salt, and ½ teaspoon pepper. Dredge chicken in flour mixture, coating well. Sauté in butter in a large skillet until golden brown. Transfer chicken to a shallow 2-quart casserole, and add water to cover. Reserve pan drippings in skillet; set aside. Bake chicken at 350° for 50 minutes or until tender. Remove chicken to serving platter, and keep warm.

Add ¾ cup half-and-half to pan drippings, stirring until smooth. Combine remaining half-and-half and 1 tablespoon flour, mixing well. Stir into pan dripping mixture. Cook mixture over medium heat, stirring constantly, until thickened and bubbly. Stir in salt and pepper to taste. Serve gravy over chicken. Yield: 4 to 6 servings.

CHICKEN ÉTOUFFÉE

1 (5- to 5½-pound) baking hen
4 strips bacon, cut into ½-inch pieces
1 lemon, thinly sliced
2 carrots, scraped and cut into 2-inch pieces
2 medium onions, coarsely chopped
1 teaspoon dried whole thyme
1 teaspoon chopped fresh parsley
1 bay leaf, crushed
1 cup water
1 cup chicken broth
½ teaspoon salt
¼ teaspoon pepper

Remove giblets from cavity of chicken, and reserve for other uses. Rinse chicken with cold water, and pat dry. Tie ends of legs to tail with string. Lift wingtips up and over back so they are tucked under chicken securely.

Combine remaining ingredients in a large Dutch oven; place chicken on top of other ingredients. Cover and simmer for 1 hour and 45 minutes.

Cut the cord holding the drumstick ends to the tail; this will ensure that the inside of the thighs are cooked. Cover and simmer an additional 30 minutes or until drumsticks are easy to move. Remove chicken, and baste well with pan drippings. Transfer chicken and vegetables to a serving platter. Yield: 4 to 6 servings.

STAR ATTRACTIONS

Center Stage for Southern Poultry

To reformulate an old question, which came first, the chicken or history? The Greeks had chickens from Asia by the 6th century B.C. The Romans were quick to pick up on a good thing, and some credit them with "inventing" the capon. According to legend, a powerful Roman politician lost so much sleep because of the roosters' crowing in his neighborhood that he ordered them neutered. On our side of the globe, the Aztecs kept chickens as far back as can be ascertained. In primitive societies, the cock was frequently used as a sacrifice and for divination.

By the 1600s, chicken was dear in England; the appearance of the bird on one's table was a sign of some affluence. This was the state of affairs when the colonists sailed from Britain. Roast chicken has lost none of its savor; perhaps it has even gained some through breeding and our choices of stuffings.

The turkey in America goes back even further, some ten million years according to fossil evidence, and was among the exotic fauna collected and taken back to Europe by Columbus and Cortez.

England, Italy, and France had been raising turkeys from New World stock since 1530, so the colonists knew what to do when they spotted a turkey: fire away. They found the Eastern Wild Turkey quite different from the domesticated bird they knew. This bird was a powerful flyer, could glide for a mile without flapping a wing, and was a tough, sinewy beast when trussed for cooking. Some of our colonial recipes call for boiling or stewing, not roasting, turkey. Instructions generally call for sewing the stuffed bird up inside a domestic (muslin) bag before placing in the stewing kettle. This method produced a tenderer fowl than one roasted before an open fire, the alternative method before ovens came in. Years of cross-breeding the wild turkey with tame stock brought from Europe resulted at last in today's broad-breasted bronze superbird with more and juicier meat per pound of bone. But the turkey has remained the focal point of our traditional Thanksgiving Dinners as well as other special occasions celebrated by our forefathers.

A royal feast by any standard. Dinner begins with tureen of Creamed Oysters with Virginia Ham. Platter holds Turkey with Chestnut Stuffing and Acorn Squash with Cranberries. Southern Broccoli, Creamed Onions, Corn Sticks, and Carolina Apple Pie complete the feast.

PLANTATION HARVEST FEAST

Patriotic Benjamin Franklin never got over his snit when the American Bald Eagle defeated his candidate, the turkey, as the official United States bird. The bald eagle, in Franklin's words, was a "...bird of bad moral character...the turkey is a much more respectable bird and withal a true native of America." Certainly the early colonists would have agreed with Ben Franklin, for the wild turkey was one of the first meats to grace their table.

The harvest (or Thanksgiving) dinner on these pages reflects foods whose existence in Colonial times has been verified through sources such as gardening records and rare books at the Colonial Williamsburg Research Center, and John Smith's 1624 *Generall Historie of Virginia.*

CREAMED OYSTERS WITH VIRGINIA HAM
ROAST TURKEY WITH CHESTNUT STUFFING
CREAMED ONIONS
ACORN SQUASH WITH CRANBERRIES
SOUTHERN BROCCOLI
CORN STICKS
OLD VIRGINIA SALLY LUNN
CAROLINA APPLE PIE

Serves 8

The Metropolitan Museum of Art, Gift of Edgar and Bernice Chrysler Garbisch

CREAMED OYSTERS WITH VIRGINIA HAM

3 (12-ounce) containers fresh
  Select oysters, undrained
¼ cup butter or margarine
¼ cup all-purpose flour
2 cups whipping cream
¼ cup sherry
1 pound cooked country ham,
  diced
½ teaspoon salt
¼ teaspoon pepper
Toast points

Drain oysters, reserving ½ cup oyster liquor; set aside.

Melt butter in a Dutch oven over low heat; add flour, stirring until smooth. Cook 1 minute, stirring constantly. Gradually add reserved oyster liquor, whipping cream, and sherry; cook over medium heat, stirring constantly, until thickened and bubbly.

Add oysters, ham, salt, and pepper; cook over low heat 10 minutes, stirring frequently. Serve over toast points. Yield: 8 servings.

ROAST TURKEY WITH CHESTNUT STUFFING

1 (12- to 13-pound) turkey
Chestnut Stuffing
3 tablespoons vegetable oil
Giblet Gravy (See page 49)

Remove giblets and neck from turkey; reserve for Giblet Gravy. Rinse turkey thoroughly with cold water, and pat dry. Cover and refrigerate while preparing stuffing.

Stuff Chestnut Stuffing into cavity of turkey and close cavity with skewers. Tie ends of legs to tail with string or tuck them under band of skin at tail. Lift wingtips up and over back, tucking under bird securely.

Brush entire bird with vegetable oil, and place breast side up in a roasting pan. Insert meat thermometer in breast or meaty part of thigh, making sure it does not touch bone. Bake at 325° for 3½ hours, basting frequently with pan drippings. Cut the string or band of skin holding the drumstick ends to the tail. Continue baking an additional 30 minutes to 1 hour until drumsticks are easy to move, or meat thermometer registers 185°. If turkey gets too brown, cover lightly with aluminum foil.

Transfer turkey to serving platter. Skim fat from pan drippings and discard fat. Reserve pan drippings for Giblet Gravy. Let turkey stand 15 minutes before carving. Serve with Giblet Gravy. Yield: 16 to 24 servings.

Chestnut Stuffing:

1½ pounds raw chestnuts
1 cup butter or margarine
1½ cups chopped celery
1 medium onion, chopped
2 teaspoons salt
1 teaspoon dried whole thyme
1 teaspoon ground marjoram
½ teaspoon pepper
8 cups soft breadcrumbs

Place chestnuts in a medium saucepan; cover with water, and bring to a boil. Reduce heat to medium, and cook 10 to 15 minutes. Remove 3 or 4 chestnuts from water; immediately cut each chestnut in half and remove outer shell and inner skin. Repeat procedure with remaining chestnuts; discard cooking liquid. Chop chestnuts; set aside.

Melt butter in a large Dutch oven over low heat. Add celery, onion, salt, thyme, marjoram, and pepper, stirring well. Cook over medium heat 10 minutes, stirring frequently. Remove from heat; gradually add breadcrumbs and chestnuts, stirring until well combined. Yield: 9 cups (enough for a 12-pound turkey).

Sailing ship passes estate in Tidewater, Virginia. American primitive, The Plantation, c.1825. Artist unknown.

CREAMED ONIONS

34 small boiling onions
1 teaspoon salt, divided
¼ cup butter or margarine
¼ cup plus 1 tablespoon all-purpose flour
2 cups milk
⅛ teaspoon hot sauce
¼ cup slivered almonds, toasted

Peel onions; place in a large saucepan. Cover with water; sprinkle with ½ teaspoon salt, and bring to a boil. Reduce heat, and cook 20 minutes or until tender. Drain well, and place onions in a 2-quart casserole.

Melt butter in a heavy saucepan over low heat; add flour and remaining salt, stirring until smooth. Cook 1 minute, stirring constantly. Gradually add milk; cook over medium heat, stirring constantly, until thickened and bubbly. Stir in hot sauce. Pour cream mixture over onions. Sprinkle with almonds. Yield: 8 servings.

ACORN SQUASH WITH CRANBERRIES

4 medium acorn squash
1½ cups fresh cranberries
1 cup firmly packed brown sugar
¼ cup butter or margarine, melted
1 teaspoon ground cinnamon

Cut squash in half lengthwise, and remove seeds; set aside. Wash cranberries and drain. Combine cranberries and remaining ingredients, tossing lightly.

Spoon cranberry mixture evenly into squash halves. Place in a 13- x 9- x 2-inch baking dish, and add ½ inch water. Bake, uncovered, at 350° for 1 hour and 20 minutes. Yield: 8 servings.

SOUTHERN BROCCOLI

3 pounds fresh broccoli
½ cup shortening
¼ cup plus 1 tablespoon
 water
2 teaspoons salt
2 tablespoons lemon juice
Lemon rind curls (optional)

Trim off large leaves of broccoli. Remove tough ends of lower stalks, and wash broccoli thoroughly. Separate into spears; coarsely chop stalks and flowerets.

Heat shortening in a heavy skillet. Add broccoli, water, and salt; stir well. Cover, and cook over medium heat 13 minutes, stirring occasionally. Remove from heat, and sprinkle with lemon juice. Garnish with lemon rind curls, if desired. Yield: 8 servings.

CORN STICKS

⅓ cup butter or margarine,
 softened
⅓ cup sugar
3 eggs
2⅔ cups cornmeal
2 cups sifted cake flour
2 tablespoons baking powder
1½ teaspoons salt
2⅓ cups milk

Cream butter; gradually add sugar, beating until light and fluffy. Add eggs, one at a time, beating well after each addition.

Combine cornmeal, flour, baking powder, and salt; add to creamed mixture alternately with milk, beginning and ending with cornmeal mixture.

Place a well-greased cast-iron cornstick pan in a 400° oven for 3 minutes or until hot. Remove from oven, and spoon batter into pan, filling two-thirds full. Bake at 400° for 20 minutes or until lightly browned. Yield: about 2 dozen.

OLD VIRGINIA SALLY LUNN

4¼ cups all-purpose flour,
 divided
¼ cup sugar
1 package dry yeast
1 teaspoon salt
¾ cup milk
¼ cup water
¼ cup shortening
¼ cup butter
3 eggs

Combine 2 cups flour, sugar, yeast, and salt in a large mixing bowl; stir well.

Combine milk, water, shortening, and butter in a medium saucepan. Heat mixture to 120° to 130°; shortening and butter do not need to melt. Add to flour mixture, stirring well. Add eggs; beat at low speed with electric mixer until moistened. Increase speed to medium, and beat an additional 3 minutes. Gradually stir in enough remaining flour to make a stiff batter. Cover, and let rise in a warm place (85°), free from drafts, 1 hour or until doubled in bulk.

Stir batter, and spoon into a greased 10-inch tube pan. Cover, and let rise in a warm place (85°), free from drafts, 30 minutes or until doubled in bulk.

Bake at 350° for 45 minutes or until golden brown. Remove bread from pan. Serve warm or place on a wire rack to cool. Yield: one 10-inch loaf.

Note: Batter may be baked in a Bundt pan for a more attractive loaf.

Ceramic Bundt pan, c.1825.

The Museum of Early Southern Decorative Arts

CAROLINA APPLE PIE

Double-Crust Pastry
¾ cup sugar
2 tablespoons all-purpose
 flour
1 teaspoon grated lemon
 rind
½ teaspoon ground
 cinnamon
Pinch of salt
5 medium Granny Smith
 apples, peeled, cored, and
 thinly sliced
2 tablespoons butter or
 margarine
1 egg white, slightly beaten

Line a 9-inch pieplate with half of pastry. Combine sugar, flour, rind, cinnamon, and salt; stir well. Sprinkle one-third of mixture into pastry shell. Top with apple slices. Sprinkle remaining sugar mixture over apples; dot with butter.

Cover with top crust, and slit in several places to allow steam to escape; seal and flute edges. Brush pastry lightly with beaten egg white. Bake at 450° for 10 minutes; reduce heat to 375°, and bake an additional 30 minutes. Yield: one 9-inch pie.

Double-Crust Pastry:

2 cups all-purpose flour
½ teaspoon salt
⅔ cup lard
5 to 6 tablespoons cold water

Combine flour and salt; cut in lard with pastry blender until mixture resembles coarse meal. Sprinkle cold water evenly over surface; stir with a fork until dry ingredients are moistened. Shape dough into a ball; chill. Divide in half, and roll each portion to ⅛-inch thickness on a lightly floured surface. Yield: pastry for one double-crust 9-inch pie.

TURKEY, AN ALL-AMERICAN FAVORITE

BASIC ROAST TURKEY

1 (11½- to 12-pound) turkey

Remove giblets and neck from turkey; reserve for other uses. Rinse turkey thoroughly with cold water; pat dry.

Close cavity of turkey with skewers. Tie ends of legs to tail with string or tuck them under band of skin at tail. Lift wingtips up and over back, tucking under bird securely.

Place turkey, breast side up, on a rack in a roasting pan. Insert meat thermometer in breast or meaty part of thigh, making sure it does not touch bone. Cover turkey lightly with aluminum foil. Bake at 325° for 3½ hours; remove aluminum foil. Cut the string or band of skin holding the drumstick ends to the tail; this will ensure that the insides of the thighs are cooked. Bake an additional 30 minutes until drumsticks are easy to move or meat thermometer registers 185°.

Transfer turkey to serving platter. Let stand 15 minutes before carving. Yield: 16 to 24 servings.

ROAST TURKEY WITH SAUSAGE-CORNBREAD DRESSING

1 (12- to 14-pound) turkey
Sausage-Cornbread
  Dressing
2 tablespoons butter or
  margarine, melted
½ teaspoon salt
½ teaspoon pepper
2 tablespoons all-purpose
  flour
2 cups water
Cranberry sauce (optional)

Remove giblets and neck from turkey; set aside. Rinse turkey thoroughly with cold water; pat dry. Cover and refrigerate while preparing dressing.

Stuff Sausage-Cornbread Dressing into cavity of turkey; close with skewers. Tie ends of legs to tail with string or tuck them under band of skin at tail. Lift wingtips up and over back, tucking under bird securely.

Brush entire bird with melted butter; sprinkle with salt and pepper. Rub flour over surface of turkey. Place breast side up on a rack in a roasting pan; pour 2 cups water in bottom of pan. Bake at 450° for 30 minutes; reduce heat to 325° and bake 3 hours. Cut the string or band of skin holding the drumstick ends to the tail. Continue baking an additional 30 minutes to 1 hour or until drumsticks are easy to move. If turkey gets too brown, cover lightly with aluminum foil.

Transfer turkey to platter. Let stand at least 15 minutes before carving. Serve with cranberry sauce, if desired. Yield: 16 to 24 servings.

Sausage-Cornbread Dressing:

2 cups cold water
6 cups cornbread crumbs
6 slices bread, cut into
  1-inch cubes
¼ cup water
½ teaspoon salt
½ teaspoon pepper
½ cup butter or margarine
½ pound bulk pork
  sausage
2 cups chopped celery
1 medium onion, finely
  chopped

Place reserved giblets in saucepan with water; cover, and simmer 1 to 2 hours or until giblets are tender. Remove from broth, reserving 1 cup broth. Chop giblets; set aside.

Combine cornbread and bread cubes in a large mixing bowl; add water, salt, and pepper. Set aside.

Melt butter in a large skillet; add sausage, celery, and onion. Sauté 3 minutes. Cover, and cook an additional 30 minutes or until sausage is browned and vegetables are tender; stir frequently. Remove from heat; stir into bread mixture. Add reserved giblet broth and giblets, mixing well. Yield: 9 cups (enough for a 12-pound turkey).

A nineteenth-century advertising card invites inspection of "other side."

APRICOT BRANDY
CORDIAL

ROAST TURKEY IN WINE AND BRANDY

1 (12- to 13-pound) turkey
1 teaspoon salt
1 teaspoon pepper
¼ cup butter or margarine, melted
¼ cup Chablis or other dry white wine
¼ cup apricot-flavored brandy
1 teaspoon dried whole thyme
1 teaspoon dried whole basil

Remove giblets and neck from turkey; reserve for other uses. Rinse turkey thoroughly with cold water; pat dry. Combine salt and pepper; sprinkle inside cavity of turkey. Close cavity of turkey with skewers. Tie ends of legs to tail with string or tuck them under band of skin at tail. Lift wingtips up and over back, tucking under bird securely.

Brush entire bird with melted butter; place breast side up in a shallow roasting pan.

Combine remaining ingredients, stirring well; pour over turkey. Insert meat thermometer in breast or meaty part of thigh, making sure it does not touch bone. Bake at 325° for 3 hours, basting frequently with pan drippings. Cut the string or band of skin holding the drumstick ends to the tail. Continue baking an additional 1 to 1½ hours until drumsticks are easy to move or meat thermometer registers 185°. If turkey gets too brown, cover lightly with aluminum foil. Transfer turkey to serving platter. Let stand 15 minutes before carving. Yield: 16 to 24 servings.

ROAST TURKEY WITH RAISIN STUFFING

1 (17- to 17½-pound) turkey
2 teaspoons salt
2 teaspoons pepper
Raisin Stuffing
½ cup butter or margarine, melted and divided
Red and green grapes (optional)
Fresh parsley sprigs (optional)

Remove giblets and neck from turkey; reserve for other uses. Rinse turkey thoroughly with cold water; pat dry. Combine salt and pepper; sprinkle over surface and in cavity of turkey.

Stuff Raisin Stuffing into cavity of turkey; close with skewers. Tie ends of legs to tail with string or tuck them under band of skin at tail. Lift wingtips up and over back, tucking under bird securely.

Brush entire bird with ¼ cup melted butter; place breast side up on a rack in a roasting pan. Insert meat thermometer in breast or meaty part of thigh, making sure it does not touch bone. Bake at 325° for 3 hours, basting frequently with remaining butter. Cut the string or band of skin holding drumstick ends to the tail. Continue baking an additional 1 to 1½ hours until drumsticks are easy to move or meat thermometer registers 185°. If turkey gets too brown, cover lightly with aluminum foil.

Transfer turkey to serving platter. Let stand 15 minutes before carving. Garnish with grapes and parsley, if desired. Yield: about 20 to 30 servings.

Raisin Stuffing:

1 pound ground beef
1 (15-ounce) package raisins
1 small onion, chopped
1 tablespoon butter or margarine
1 tablespoon chopped fresh parsley
1 teaspoon ground thyme
5½ cups cracker crumbs
1 egg, beaten
2 tablespoons Worcestershire sauce
1 teaspoon salt
¼ teaspoon pepper

Combine first 6 ingredients in a Dutch oven; cook over medium heat, stirring occasionally, until beef is browned and onion is tender. Add remaining ingredients; stir well. Yield: 10 cups (enough for a 17-pound turkey).

In roasting meat before an open fire, as it was historically done, only one side of the meat at a time was exposed to the fire while the rest cooled in the open air. The reflector oven or "tin kitchen," as it was called, was a welcome addition to the cook's *batterie de cuisine*. It was shaped like a drum, with one side open toward the fire, with a spit running through and a crank for turning. While part of the meat was roasting, the part away from the fire stayed warm, hastening the cooking and effecting a saving in fuel. A hinged door could be opened at the back of the drum to allow for basting the meat each time the spit was turned. The tin kitchen was by no means an oven as we know it. It was made for roasting; the closed oven is a baking unit containing steam, and there lies the difference between roasting and baking. A closed oven, even when we are "dry-roasting," keeps steam hovering around the meat, whereas in spit-roasting, the steam is dissipated into the surrounding air. The oven has turned our roast turkey into a baked one.

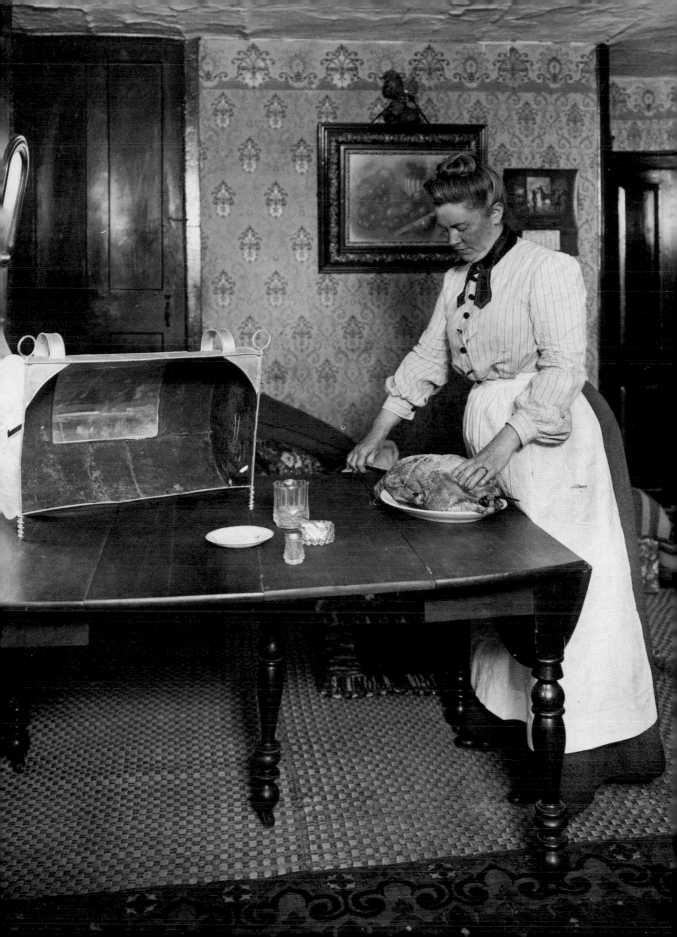

Oven-Barbecued Turkey

OVEN-BARBECUED TURKEY

1 (10- to 11-pound) turkey
2 tablespoons olive oil
2 teaspoons salt
2 teaspoons pepper
Barbecue Sauce
Red and green pepper rings
   (optional)
Fresh parsley sprigs (optional)

Remove giblets and neck from turkey; reserve for other uses. Rinse turkey thoroughly with cold water; pat dry. Rub turkey with olive oil. Combine salt and pepper; sprinkle over surface and in cavity of turkey.

Close cavity of turkey with skewers. Tie ends of legs to tail with string or tuck them under band of skin at tail. Lift wingtips up and over back, tucking under bird securely.

Place turkey, breast side up, in a deep roasting pan. Bake at 350° for 2 hours, basting frequently with pan drippings.

Cut the cord or band of skin holding the drumstick ends to the tail. Pour Barbecue Sauce over the turkey. Cover, and bake an additional hour, basting frequently with Barbecue Sauce. Turkey is done when drumsticks are easy to move.

Transfer turkey to serving platter. Let stand 15 minutes before carving. Garnish with pepper rings and parsley, if desired. Yield: 10 to 12 servings.

Barbecue Sauce:

1 (14½-ounce) can whole
   tomatoes, undrained
1 medium onion, sliced
2 cloves garlic, minced
3 fresh celery leaves, chopped
1 bay leaf
1 teaspoon sugar
1 teaspoon salt
¼ teaspoon chili powder
¼ teaspoon paprika
⅛ teaspoon dried whole
   thyme
⅛ teaspoon dried whole basil
1 medium onion, chopped
1 medium-size green pepper,
   chopped
2 tablespoons olive oil
1 tablespoon all-purpose flour
4 drops hot sauce
Dash of soy sauce
1 whole pimiento, chopped

Combine first 11 ingredients in a Dutch oven; bring to a boil. Reduce heat; cover, and cook over low heat 25 minutes or until vegetables are tender. Remove from heat, and process mixture through a food mill. Return tomato mixture to Dutch oven, and set aside.

Sauté chopped onion and green pepper in olive oil until tender; stir in remaining ingredients. Add sautéed vegetable mixture to reserved tomato mixture, stirring until well combined. Yield: about 2 quarts.

SMOKED TURKEY

1 (13- to 14-pound) turkey
¼ cup butter or margarine,
   softened
1 tablespoon coarsely ground
   black pepper
1 teaspoon seasoned salt
1 teaspoon celery salt
½ teaspoon red pepper
4 carrots, cut into 2-inch
   pieces
4 stalks celery, halved
2 medium apples, quartered
2 medium onions, quartered
1 cup Chablis or other dry
   white wine
1 teaspoon fines herbes
1 teaspoon dried whole
   rosemary
2 bay leaves

Remove giblets and neck from turkey; reserve for other uses. Rinse turkey thoroughly with cold water; pat dry. Rub butter over surface of turkey. Combine black pepper, seasoned salt, and celery salt; sprinkle over surface and in cavity of turkey. Sprinkle red pepper over surface.

Stuff carrots, celery, apples, and onions in cavity of turkey; close cavity with skewers. Tie ends of tail with string or tuck them under band of skin at tail. Lift wingtips up and over back, tucking under bird securely. Set aside.

Combine wine and remaining seasonings; stir well. Set aside.

Prepare charcoal fire in smoker, and let burn 10 to 15 minutes. Place water pan in smoker, and fill with wine mixture. Add enough hot water to fill pan, if necessary.

Place turkey on food rack. Cover with smoker lid; cook about 16 hours, refilling water pan with additional water, if needed. Turkey is done when drumsticks are easy to move.

Transfer turkey to a serving platter; discard vegetables. Let stand at least 15 minutes before carving. Yield: about 17 to 26 servings.

CHICKEN EVERY SUNDAY

BASIC BAKED CHICKEN

1 (2- to 2½-pound)
   broiler-fryer
1 teaspoon salt, divided

Remove giblets from cavity of chicken; reserve for other uses. Rinse chicken with cold water, and pat dry. Sprinkle ½ teaspoon salt inside cavity of chicken. Lift wingtips up and over back, tucking under bird. Truss chicken, and place on a rack, breast side up, in a shallow roasting pan. Sprinkle outside of chicken with remaining ½ teaspoon salt. Bake at 350° for 1 hour or until drumsticks are easy to move and juices run clear. Yield: 4 servings.

*The all-American,
all-purpose Plymouth
Rock. Comes in
white, buff, and barred.
These are Barred Rocks.*

COLONIAL ROAST CHICKEN WITH CELERY STUFFING

1 (3½- to 4-pound)
   broiler-fryer
1 cup chopped celery
1 medium onion, chopped
¼ cup butter or margarine
2 cups toasted soft
   breadcrumbs
1 cup cornbread crumbs
¾ cup chicken broth
½ teaspoon salt
½ teaspoon rubbed sage
¼ teaspoon pepper
1 lemon, halved
¼ cup honey
¼ cup apple butter

Remove giblets and neck from chicken; reserve for other uses. Rinse chicken thoroughly with cold water; pat dry. Fold neck skin over back, and secure with a wooden pick.

Sauté celery and onion in butter until tender. Combine the sautéed vegetables, toasted breadcrumbs, cornbread, broth, salt, sage, and pepper in a large mixing bowl; stir until well blended.

Place stuffing in cavity of chicken; close cavity with skewers. Tie ends of legs to tail with string. Lift wingtips up and over back, tucking under bird securely.

Place bird, breast side up, in a shallow roasting pan. Rub surface of chicken with lemon halves. Combine honey and apple butter, stirring well to make glaze. Brush chicken with glaze. Bake at 325° for 1 hour or until drumsticks are easy to move and juices run clear. Baste occasionally with glaze. Yield: 4 servings.

ROAST CHICKEN WITH SHRIMP STUFFING

1 (3½- to 4-pound) broiler-fryer
½ pound shrimp, peeled, deveined, and chopped
¼ cup chopped onion
¼ cup plus 1 tablespoon butter or margarine, divided
1 egg
2½ teaspoons salt, divided
½ teaspoon ground thyme
1⅛ teaspoons pepper, divided
3 cups soft breadcrumbs
2 tablespoons milk
3 cups water
3 tablespoons all-purpose flour

Remove giblets and neck from chicken. Chop giblets; set aside. Rinse chicken with cold water; pat dry. Fold neck skin of chicken over back; secure with a wooden pick. Lift wingtips up and over back, tucking under bird securely. Set aside.

Sauté shrimp and onion in 3 tablespoons butter until tender. Combine shrimp mixture, egg, ½ teaspoon salt, thyme, ⅛ teaspoon pepper, breadcrumbs, and milk, stirring well; stuff cavity of chicken with mixture. Close cavity, and secure with wooden picks; truss.

Place chicken, breast side up, in a shallow roasting pan. Add remaining butter, salt, pepper, and water to pan. Bake at 350° for 1 hour; add chopped giblets to pan drippings. Bake 30 minutes or until drumsticks are easy to move. Remove chicken to serving platter; keep warm. Reserve drippings.

Sprinkle flour evenly in a 10-inch cast-iron skillet; place over medium heat. Brown flour by constantly stirring with a wooden spoon. Combine browned flour and 3 tablespoons drippings in a medium saucepan, mixing well; stir into remaining pan drippings. Cook the mixture over medium-high heat, stirring constantly, until thickened and bubbly. Serve gravy with chicken and stuffing. Yield: 4 servings.

FESTIVE ROAST CHICKEN WITH TENNESSEE COUNTRY SAUSAGE STUFFING

1 (5½- to 6-pound) baking hen
Tennessee Country Sausage Stuffing
2 tablespoons vegetable oil
1 (29-ounce) can peach halves, drained (optional)
1 (18-ounce) jar spiced crabapples, drained (optional)
Fresh parsley sprigs (optional)

Remove giblets and neck from hen; reserve for other uses. Rinse hen thoroughly with cold water; pat dry.

Spoon Tennessee Country Sausage Stuffing lightly into neck cavity. Fold neck skin over stuffing; secure with a skewer. Lift wingtips up and over back, tucking under bird securely.

Spoon Tennessee Country Sausage Stuffing lightly into body cavity of hen, and secure with skewers; truss. Tie ends of legs to tail with string.

Place hen, breast side up, in a roasting pan; brush entire bird with oil. Insert meat thermometer in breast or meaty part of thigh, making sure it does not touch bone. Bake at 325° for 2½ hours until meat thermometer registers 185° or until drumsticks are easy to move. Baste hen occasionally with pan drippings. If hen gets too brown, cover lightly with foil.

Transfer hen to serving platter; keep warm. Let stand 15 minutes before carving. Garnish with peach halves, crabapples, and parsley, if desired. Yield: 4 to 6 servings.

Tennessee Country Sausage Stuffing:

1 pound raw chestnuts
1 tablespoon butter or margarine
¾ cup chicken broth
1 tablespoon Madeira or other dry red wine
¼ pound Tennessee smoked country sausage
2 medium onions, chopped
¾ cup chopped celery
3 cups soft breadcrumbs
½ teaspoon dried whole thyme
½ teaspoon salt
¼ teaspoon rubbed sage
⅛ teaspoon pepper
2 tablespoons chopped fresh parsley

Place chestnuts and water to cover in a medium sauce pan; bring to a boil. Reduce heat to medium, and cook 10 to 15 minutes. Remove 3 or 4 chestnuts from water; immediately cut each chestnut in half, and remove outer shell and inner skin. Repeat procedure with remaining chestnuts; discard cooking liquid.

Place chestnuts in a medium-size Dutch oven; add butter, broth, and wine. Cook over low heat for 35 minutes or until liquid is absorbed.

Brown sausage in a heavy skillet; remove sausage to drain, reserving drippings in skillet. Add onion and celery to skillet; sauté until tender. Add sausage, sautéed vegetables, and remaining ingredients to chestnut mixture in Dutch oven; stir until well blended.

Stuff chicken; place any remaining stuffing in a lightly greased 1-quart casserole. Bake at 325° for 30 minutes or until thoroughly heated. Yield: 6 cups (enough for a 6-pound hen).

Sausage Stuffer, 1858

Roast Capon with Virginia Oyster Stuffing: a pretty plate.

ROAST CAPON
WITH VIRGINIA OYSTER STUFFING

1 (8- to 8½-pound) capon
1 teaspoon salt
¼ cup plus 2 tablespoons
 butter or margarine
4 medium onions, chopped
1 cup finely chopped celery
5 cups herb-seasoned
 croutons
½ cup chicken broth
¼ cup chopped fresh parsley
1 tablespoon Worcestershire
 sauce
½ teaspoon salt
½ teaspoon pepper
½ teaspoon rubbed sage
¼ teaspoon dried whole
 thyme
¼ teaspoon dry mustard
1 (12-ounce) container fresh
 Select oysters, drained and
 quartered
2 tablespoons vegetable oil
Spiced peaches (optional)
Fresh parsley sprigs (optional)

Remove giblets and neck from capon; reserve for other uses. Rinse capon thoroughly with cold water; pat dry. Sprinkle 1 teaspoon salt over surface and in cavity of capon.

Melt butter in a large skillet; sauté onion and celery until transparent. Remove from heat; stir in next 9 ingredients, mixing well. Stir oysters into stuffing mixture.

Place stuffing in cavity of capon; close with skewers. Tie ends of legs to tail with string or tuck them under flap of skin around tail. Lift wingtips up and over back, tucking under bird securely.

Brush entire bird with oil; place breast side up in a roasting pan. Insert meat thermometer in breast or meaty part of thigh, making sure it does not touch bone. Bake, covered, at 325° for 3 hours. Remove cover, and bake an additional 30 minutes until meat thermometer registers 185° or drumsticks are easy to move.

Transfer capon to serving platter. Let stand 15 minutes before carving. Garnish with spiced peaches and parsley, if desired. Yield: 4 to 6 servings.

BAKED CHICKEN
IN SCUPPERNONG
WINE

1 (3½- to 4-pound)
 broiler-fryer
2 cups Scuppernong wine
2 teaspoons ground nutmeg
½ teaspoon salt
¼ teaspoon pepper
2 tablespoons all-purpose
 flour
Red and green grapes
 (optional)

Remove giblets and neck from chicken, and reserve for other uses. Rinse chicken with cold water, and pat dry. Fold neck skin of chicken over back, and secure with a wooden pick. Lift wingtips up and over back, tucking under bird securely. Close cavity of chicken with skewers; truss. Place chicken, breast side up, on a rack in a shallow roasting pan. Bake at 350° for 1 hour or until drumsticks are easy to move and juices run clear.

Combine wine, nutmeg, salt, and pepper; pour over chicken. Bake an additional 30 minutes, basting occasionally. Remove chicken to a serving platter, and keep warm. Reserve 1 cup pan drippings.

Blend flour with a small amount of water, mixing to form a smooth paste; stir into pan drippings. Cook over medium heat, stirring constantly, until thickened and bubbly. Garnish with grape clusters around chicken, if desired. Serve with gravy. Yield: 4 to 6 servings.

ROAST CORNISH HENS WITH SAGE STUFFING

6 (1- to 1½-pound) Cornish hens
½ lemon
1½ teaspoons salt
¾ teaspoon pepper
3 chicken livers (about ¼ pound)
¼ cup plus 1 tablespoon butter or margarine, divided
¼ cup chopped onion
½ cup chopped cooked ham
1¼ cups sliced fresh mushrooms
¼ cup slivered almonds
¼ cup chopped fresh parsley
2¼ cups Chablis or other dry white wine, divided
2 cups soft breadcrumbs
½ teaspoon rubbed sage
¼ teaspoon dried whole thyme
½ cup red currant jelly
¼ cup butter or margarine
2 tablespoons all-purpose flour

An 1800s card when opened (below) gives glimpse of roasting chickens in "Eureka" cooker.

Staples & Charles

Remove giblets from hens. Reserve livers for stuffing; discard giblets. Rinse hens with cold water; pat dry. Rub cavity of each with lemon. Sprinkle each cavity with ¼ teaspoon salt and ⅛ teaspoon pepper.

Combine reserved livers and chicken livers in a colander; rinse thoroughly, and pat dry. Sauté livers in 3 tablespoons butter in a medium skillet 3 minutes or until livers are browned. Remove livers; chop finely and set aside. Reserve drippings in skillet.

Add 2 tablespoons butter, onion, and ham to skillet; sauté 5 minutes. Add chopped liver, mushrooms, almonds, parsley, and ¾ cup wine; simmer 3 minutes. Remove from heat, and add breadcrumbs, sage, and thyme, stirring well. Stuff hens lightly with herb mixture. Close cavities, and secure with wooden picks; truss. Place hens, breast side up, in a shallow baking pan.

Combine jelly and remaining ¼ cup butter in a small saucepan; cook over low heat, stirring often, until jelly melts. Stir in 1 cup wine. Pour mixture over hens. Bake at 400° for 20 minutes; reduce heat to 350°, and bake an additional 45 minutes, basting occasionally. If hens get too brown, cover loosely with aluminum foil.

Skim fat from pan drippings. Discard fat, and transfer drippings to a small saucepan. Blend flour with a small amount of water, mixing to form a smooth paste; stir into drippings. Add remaining wine; cook, stirring constantly, until thickened and bubbly. Serve gravy with Cornish hens. Yield: 6 servings.

SPIT-ROASTED CORNISH HENS WITH RAISIN PECAN STUFFING

½ cup raisins, chopped
⅓ cup chopped pecans
¼ cup finely chopped celery
2½ tablespoons butter or margarine, melted
¼ teaspoon dried whole rosemary
1 cup herb-seasoned stuffing mix
⅓ cup water
4 (1- to 1½-pound) Cornish hens
3 tablespoons butter or margarine, melted

Sauté raisins, pecans, and celery in 2½ tablespoons butter in a medium saucepan until celery is tender. Stir in rosemary, stuffing mix, and water; remove raisin mixture from heat.

Remove giblets from hens; reserve for other uses. Rinse hens with cold water, and pat dry. Stuff hens lightly with raisin mixture (about ⅔ cup per hen). Close cavities, and secure with wooden picks; truss.

Heat broiler-rotisserie until the heating element is red. Thread 2 hens on the spit; secure tightly with prongs at each end of the spit. Make sure hens are properly balanced to avoid strain on the motor when spit is turning. Brush hens with half of remaining melted butter. Place spit on rotisserie about 3 inches from source of heat. Turn on rotisserie motor. Bake at 400° for 1 hour or until drumsticks move easily. Repeat procedure with remaining hens and butter. Transfer hens to a serving platter, and serve warm. Yield: 4 servings.

ROAST CORNISH HENS WITH HERB GRAVY

4 (1- to 1½-pound) Cornish hens
½ cup butter or margarine, melted
½ cup instant nonfat dry milk powder
2 tablespoons all-purpose flour
¼ teaspoon salt
¼ teaspoon ground marjoram
½ teaspoon dried whole basil
1½ cups water

Remove giblets from hens; reserve for other uses. Rinse hens with cold water, and pat dry; truss. Place hens, breast side up, in a shallow baking pan; brush with melted butter. Bake at 400° for 20 minutes; reduce heat to 350°. Cover, and bake an additional 35 minutes or until tender. Transfer hens to a serving platter, and keep warm. Reserve ¼ cup pan drippings.

Combine drippings and remaining ingredients in a medium saucepan. Cook over medium-high heat, stirring constantly, until thickened and bubbly. Serve gravy with Cornish hens. Yield: 4 servings.

ROCK CORNISH HENS WITH SAUSAGE STUFFING

1½ pounds hot bulk pork sausage
3 cups chopped green onion with tops
8 slices whole wheat bread, cut into 1-inch cubes
2 eggs, beaten
½ cup chopped fresh parsley
¼ cup Chablis or other dry white wine
½ teaspoon salt
½ teaspoon pepper
12 (1- to 1½-pound) Cornish hens
Salt
1 cup butter or margarine, melted
Lemon slices (optional)
Fresh parsley sprigs (optional)

Combine sausage and onion in a large skillet; cook until sausage is browned and onion is tender. Drain well. Combine next 6 ingredients in a large mixing bowl; add sausage mixture to stuffing mixture, stirring until well combined.

Remove giblets from hens; reserve for other uses. Rinse hens with cold water, and pat dry. Sprinkle with salt. Stuff hens lightly with stuffing mixture. Close cavities, and secure with wooden picks; truss. Brush hens with melted butter, and place breast side up in a shallow roasting pan. Bake at 350° for 1¼ to 1½ hours, depending on size of hens; baste often with melted butter. Garnish with lemon slices and parsley, if desired. Yield: 12 servings.

ROCK CORNISH HENS WITH OYSTER CORNBREAD STUFFING

12 (1- to 1½-pound) Cornish hens
Salt and pepper
6 cups cornbread crumbs
3 cups soft bread cubes (about 5 slices bread, cut into 1-inch cubes)
2 cups chicken broth
1½ cups chopped onion
1 cup chopped celery
2 eggs, beaten
2 teaspoons salt
1 teaspoon poultry seasoning
¾ teaspoon pepper
1 (12-ounce) container fresh Select oysters, well drained
1 cup butter or margarine, melted

Remove giblets from hens; reserve for other uses. Rinse hens with cold water, and pat dry; sprinkle salt and pepper over surfaces and inside cavities.

Combine next 9 ingredients, stirring well. Cut oysters into quarters; add to breadcrumb mixture. Stir until well combined. Stuff hens lightly with oyster mixture. Close cavities, and secure with wooden picks; truss. Place hens, breast side up, in a shallow roasting pan.

Brush hens with butter, reserving any remaining butter for basting. Bake at 350° for 1 hour and 20 minutes, basting frequently. Yield: 12 servings.

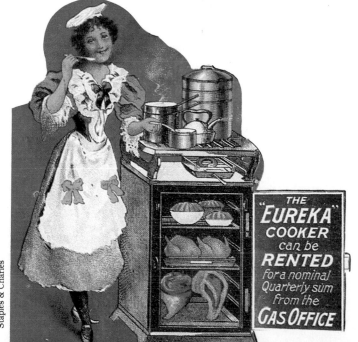

Staples & Charles

FESTIVE GAME

ROAST GOOSE WITH BAKED APPLES

1 (9½- to 10-pound) goose
1 tablespoon salt
1 teaspoon pepper
2 cloves garlic, minced
½ teaspoon ground ginger
1 medium apple, quartered
1 small onion, quartered
4 celery leaves
Additional celery leaves (optional)
Baked Apples

Remove giblets and neck from goose; reserve for other uses. Rinse goose thoroughly with cold water; pat dry. Prick fatty areas of goose with a fork at intervals. (Do not prick breast.) Lift wingtips up and over back, tucking under goose securely.

Combine salt, pepper, garlic, and ginger; rub over surface and in cavity of goose. Combine apple, onion, and 4 celery leaves. Stuff cavity with apple mixture, and close with skewers. Fold neck skin under, and place goose, breast side up, on a rack in a roasting pan. Bake, uncovered, at 400° for 30 minutes. Reduce heat to 325°, and bake an additional 2½ hours, basting occasionally with pan drippings. Goose is done when drumsticks and thighs are easy to move. Discard stuffing mixture. Transfer goose to a serving platter; garnish with celery leaves, if desired. Serve with Baked Apples surrounding goose. Yield: 6 servings.

Baked Apples:

6 medium cooking apples
3 cups cooked, mashed sweet potatoes
¼ cup butter or margarine, softened
¼ cup firmly packed brown sugar
½ teaspoon salt
½ teaspoon vanilla extract
¼ cup finely chopped pecans

Core apples to within ½ inch of bottom; peel skin from top third of each. Place apples in a shallow baking dish. Set aside.

Combine next 5 ingredients, mixing well. Stuff each apple with ½ cup sweet potato mixture. Sprinkle pecans evenly over top of each stuffed apple. Bake at 325° for 1 hour or until tender. Yield: 6 servings.

Note: Apples may be baked with goose during last hour of cooking time.

Roast goose takes kindly to baked apples stuffed with nutty sweet potatoes.

How the new cook dressed the bird.

ROAST GOOSE WITH SAUSAGE STUFFING

1 (9½- to 10-pound) goose
2 pounds bulk pork sausage
4 cups soft breadcrumbs
¾ cup chopped celery
½ cup chopped onion

Remove giblets and neck from goose; reserve for other uses. Prick fatty areas of goose with a fork at intervals. (Do not prick breast.) Combine remaining ingredients in a large mixing bowl; mix well. Stuff dressing into cavity of goose, and close cavity with skewers; truss. Lift wingtips up and over back, tucking under bird securely. Fold neck skin under, and place goose, breast side up, in a shallow roasting pan. Bake, uncovered, at 450° for 10 minutes; reduce to 350°, and bake 2 hours or until drumsticks and thighs are easy to move. Baste goose frequently with pan drippings. Yield: 6 to 8 servings.

ROAST GOOSE WITH POTATO AND PEANUT STUFFING

2 cups cooked mashed
   potatoes
1 cup fine dry breadcrumbs
1 cup dry roasted peanuts,
   finely chopped
½ cup butter or margarine,
   melted
2 tablespoons onion juice
1 teaspoon rubbed sage
1½ teaspoons salt, divided
½ teaspoon pepper
1 (10- to 10½-pound) goose
¼ cup butter or margarine,
   melted

Combine potatoes, breadcrumbs, peanuts, butter, onion juice, and sage in a medium-size mixing bowl; add ½ teaspoon salt and pepper. Stir dressing until well combined. Set aside.

Remove giblets and neck from goose; reserve for other uses. Prick fatty areas of goose with a fork at intervals. (Do not prick breast.) Stuff dressing into cavity of goose, and close cavity with skewers; truss. Sprinkle remaining salt over surface of goose. Lift wingtips up and over back, tucking under bird securely. Fold neck skin under and place goose, breast side up, in a shallow roasting pan. Bake at 375° for 2 to 2½ hours until drumsticks and thighs are easy to move. Baste goose frequently with additional melted butter. Yield: 6 to 8 servings.

ROAST DUCKLING WITH APPLE STUFFING

1 (4- to 4½-pound) dressed
   duckling
½ teaspoon salt
¼ teaspoon pepper
1 small onion, chopped
½ cup butter
3 cups soft breadcrumbs
3 cups finely chopped apples
4 eggs, beaten
½ teaspoon salt
⅛ teaspoon pepper
Celery leaves (optional)
Apple wedges (optional)

Remove giblets and neck from duckling; reserve for other uses. Rinse duckling thoroughly with cold water, and pat dry. Prick fatty areas of duckling with a fork at intervals. (Do not prick breast.) Lift wingtips up and over back, tucking under duckling securely. Combine ½ teaspoon salt and ¼ teaspoon pepper; sprinkle over surface and in cavity of duckling. Set duckling aside.

Sauté onion in butter in a large skillet until tender. Add next 5 ingredients for dressing, mixing well. Spoon dressing into cavity of duckling. Shape remaining dressing into 1½-inch balls; cover, and refrigerate. Close cavity of duckling with skewers; truss.

Fold neck skin under and place duckling, breast side up, on rack in a roasting pan. Bake, uncovered, at 325° for 2½ hours or until drumsticks and thighs are easy to move. During last 30 minutes of cooking time, place stuffing balls on rack in roasting pan. When done, transfer duckling to serving platter. Arrange stuffing balls around duckling; garnish with celery leaves and apple wedges, if desired. Yield: 4 servings.

ROAST DUCKLINGS WITH CORNBREAD STUFFING

3 cups cornbread crumbs
½ cup butter or margarine, melted
6 green onions, chopped
1 teaspoon salt
¼ teaspoon rubbed sage
½ teaspoon pepper
2 (3½- to 4-pound) dressed ducklings
1 tablespoon all-purpose flour
1 cup orange juice

Combine first 6 ingredients for stuffing. Stir well, and set aside.

Remove giblets and neck from ducklings; reserve for other uses. Rinse ducklings thoroughly with cold water; pat dry. Prick fatty areas of ducklings with a fork at intervals. (Do not prick breast.) Stuff dressing into cavity of ducklings. Close cavity with skewers; truss. Lift wingtips up and over back, tucking under bird securely. Fold neck skin under, and place ducklings, breast side up, in a roasting pan. Cover lightly with aluminum foil.

Combine flour and orange juice; mix well. Bake ducklings at 350° for 2 hours and 15 minutes, basting frequently with orange juice mixture. Yield: 6 to 8 servings.

VIRGINIA ROAST DUCKLING

1 (3½- to 4-pound) dressed duckling
¾ teaspoon salt
¼ teaspoon pepper
2 stalks celery, halved
1 medium cooking apple, quartered
1 small onion, halved

Remove giblets and neck from duckling; reserve for other uses. Rinse duckling thoroughly with cold water, and pat dry. Prick fatty areas of duckling with a fork at intervals. (Do not prick breast.) Lift wingtips up and over back, tucking under duckling securely.

Combine salt and pepper; sprinkle over surface and in cavity of duckling. Stuff cavity with celery, apple, and onion. Close cavity with skewers, and truss. Fold neck skin under, and place duckling, breast side up, on a rack in a shallow roasting pan. Bake duckling, uncovered, at 325° for 2 hours and 45 minutes or until drumsticks and thighs are easy to move. Remove duckling from oven, and discard celery, apple, and onion. Transfer duckling to serving platter. Yield: 4 servings.

DUCKLING A LA CARTE

1 (3½- to 4-pound) dressed duckling
1¾ cups red currant jelly, divided
1½ teaspoons all-purpose flour
2 cups water
2 cups claret or other red wine

Remove giblets and neck from duckling; reserve for other uses. Rinse duckling thoroughly with cold water; pat dry. Prick fatty areas of duckling with a fork at intervals. (Do not prick breast.) Fill cavity of duckling with ¾ cup currant jelly. Close cavity with skewers; truss. Lift wingtips up and over back, tucking under bird securely. Fold neck skin under, and place duckling, breast side up, in a shallow roasting pan. Sprinkle flour over duckling, and pour water into roasting pan.

Bake at 300° for 1½ hours. Combine remaining jelly and wine, mixing well. Pour wine mixture over duckling; bake 1½ hours or until drumsticks and thighs are easy to move. Baste frequently with pan drippings. Yield: about 4 servings.

John James Audubon's Hybrid Duck, *1822.*

ROAST DUCKLING WITH ORANGE SAUCE

1 (4- to 4½-pound) dressed
  duckling
1 teaspoon salt, divided
¼ teaspoon pepper
½ cup sugar
1 tablespoon red wine
  vinegar
2 tablespoons grated
  orange rind
⅔ cup orange juice
¼ cup curaçao or other
  orange-flavored liqueur
1 teaspoon lemon juice
¼ cup orange rind strips
  (optional)
Orange slices (optional)
Parsley (optional)

Remove giblets and neck from duckling; reserve for other uses. Rinse duckling thoroughly with cold water, and pat dry. Prick fatty areas of duckling with a fork at intervals. (Do not prick breast.) Lift wingtips up and over back, tucking under the duckling securely. Combine ½ teaspoon salt and ¼ teaspoon pepper; sprinkle over surface and in cavity of duckling. Close cavity with skewers, and truss. Fold neck skin under, and place duckling, breast side up, on a rack in a shallow roasting pan. Bake, uncovered, at 350° for 1¾ hours or until drumsticks and thighs are easy to move. Transfer duckling to a serving platter, and keep warm.

Skim fat from pan drippings. Discard fat, and set pan drippings aside.

Combine sugar and vinegar in a heavy skillet; bring to a boil. Reduce heat to medium high. Cook, stirring constantly, 5 minutes or until sugar is caramelized. Add grated rind, orange juice, and curaçao; simmer, stirring constantly, until sugar is dissolved. Add pan drippings; bring to a boil, and cook 1 to 2 minutes, stirring constantly. Stir in lemon juice and orange rind strips, if desired. Pour sauce over duckling. Garnish with orange slices and parsley, if desired. Yield: 4 servings.

Nineteenth-century postcard

ROAST DUCKLINGS SUPREME

2 (3½- to 4-pound) dressed
  ducklings
8 strips of orange rind
1 small onion, thinly
  sliced
1 cup thinly sliced carrots
Juice of 1 orange
1 (10-ounce) jar red currant
  jelly
Toast points

Remove giblets and neck from ducklings; reserve for other uses. Rinse ducklings thoroughly with cold water, and pat dry. Prick fatty areas of ducklings with a fork at intervals. (Do not prick breast.) Close cavity with wooden picks; truss. Lift wingtips up and over back, tucking under bird securely. Fold neck skin under and place ducklings, breast side up, on a rack in a large roasting pan. Bake ducklings at 350° for 1 hour and 20 minutes or until drumsticks and thighs are easy to move.

Skim fat from pan drippings; reserve ⅓ cup fat and discard drippings. Transfer ducklings to serving platter. Set aside, and keep warm.

Place orange rind in a small saucepan, and cover with water; bring to a boil. Reduce heat; cover, and simmer 5 minutes. Drain off water.

Sauté onion and carrots in reserved fat. Add strips of orange rind, orange juice, and currant jelly to sautéed mixture. Cook over medium heat, stirring constantly until jelly melts. Drizzle glaze over ducklings. Arrange glazed vegetables and toast points around ducklings. Yield: 6 to 8 servings.

1882 cartoon portrays the Blue Grass Club hunting duck.

ROAST DUCKLINGS BIGARADE

3 (4- to 4½-pound) dressed
  ducklings
¼ cup plus 2 tablespoons
  butter or margarine, melted
¼ cup plus 2 tablespoons
  lemon juice
1½ teaspoons all-purpose
  flour
3 medium-size Seville or
  bitter oranges
1½ teaspoons sugar
1 tablespoon red wine vinegar
Orange slices (optional)
Watercress (optional)

Remove giblets and neck from
ducklings; reserve for other
uses. Rinse ducklings
thoroughly with cold water; pat
dry. Prick fatty areas of ducklings with a fork at intervals.
(Do not prick breast.) Lift wingtips up and over back, tucking
under ducklings securely.

Combine butter and lemon
juice, stirring well. Place 2 tablespoons of the butter mixture inside the cavity of each duckling.
Rub outer skin of each with 2
tablespoons butter mixture. Set
remaining butter mixture aside.
Close cavity of ducklings with
skewers; truss. Fold neck under
and place ducklings, breast side
up, on a rack in a large roasting
pan. Bake, uncovered, at 425°
for 45 minutes. Brush ducklings with remaining butter
mixture. Continue baking for
an additional 45 minutes or
until drumsticks and thighs are
easy to move. Set ducklings
aside; keep warm.

Skim fat from pan drippings.
Discard fat, and place 1 cup
drippings in a medium saucepan; gradually add flour, stirring well. Cover, and cook over
medium heat, stirring constantly, until thickened and
bubbly. Set aside.

Grate 1 tablespoon orange
rind; squeeze ⅔ cup juice from
Seville oranges. Combine rind
and juice; set aside. Reserve remaining orange for garnishing
purposes, if desired.

Southerners are inveterate hunters; always have been. Thanks to the forethought of hunters and governments a century ago, conservation measures have assured a good supply of wild duck and goose for the taking. Along the Mississippi Flyway, in season, hunters wait to bag their limits. The wild duck of Arkansas and the Carolinas taken over the rice fields is considered especially succulent.

Most of us, though, confine our hunting to the supermarket, making our selection from the neatly dressed and packaged domesticated duckling, goose, and squab found in the freezer.

We are most familiar with the Giant White Peking breed of duck, marketed under the name of "Long Island Duckling." Interestingly, twelve percent of Long Island duckling comes from the Tidewater country near Urbanna, Virginia.

The goose not only vies with turkey as a holiday main dish, it is probably the most all 'round useful fowl we have. Legend informs us that the honking of geese warned the Romans of the approach of predatory Gauls in 309 B.C. Even today, Ballantine's Distillery in Scotland uses a gaggle of geese as a "Scotch Watch" burglar alarm.

GARLIC-ROASTED DUCKLING

1 (4½- to 5-pound) dressed duckling
3 cloves garlic, minced
1 teaspoon salt
¼ teaspoon ground ginger
¼ teaspoon pepper
2 tablespoons butter or margarine, melted
¼ cup all-purpose flour
3 celery leaves
1 onion, halved
1½ cups water
½ cup Sauterne or other dry white wine
2 tablespoons catsup
1 tablespoon flour
3 tablespoons water
½ cup sliced pimiento-stuffed olives
Pickled peaches (optional)

Remove giblets and neck from duckling; reserve for other uses. Rinse duckling with cold water; pat dry. Prick fatty areas of duckling with a fork at intervals. (Do not prick breast.) Lift wingtips up and over back, tucking under duckling securely. Combine next 4 ingredients. Rub over surface and in cavity of duckling. Cover, and refrigerate overnight.

Brush bird with melted butter; sprinkle with ¼ cup flour. Fold neck skin under, and place duckling, breast side up, on a rack in a roasting pan. Stuff cavity with celery leaves and onion. Close cavity with skewers. Place under broiler 2 minutes or until lightly browned.

Combine 1½ cups water, wine, and catsup, stirring well. Pour over duckling in roasting pan. Cover with foil, and bake at 375° for 1½ hours or until drumsticks and thighs are easy to move. Remove from oven; discard celery leaves and onion. Transfer duckling to serving platter; keep warm.

Skim fat from pan drippings. Discard fat, and pour pan drippings into a small saucepan; set aside. Combine 1 tablespoon flour and 3 tablespoons water, mixing to form a smooth paste; gradually add to pan drippings, stirring until smooth. Cook, stirring constantly, until thickened and bubbly. Stir in olives. Pour sauce over duckling. Garnish with pickled peaches, if desired. Yield: 4 servings.

Sprinkle sugar in a heavy saucepan; cook over medium heat, stirring constantly with a wooden spoon until sugar is melted and golden brown. Stir in vinegar and orange juice mixture. Add juice mixture to thickened broth mixture; cook over medium heat, stirring constantly, until thickened and bubbly. Transfer ducklings to serving platter; pour sauce over top. Garnish with orange slices and watercress, if desired. Yield: about 12 servings.

Note: Seville oranges provide the bitter flavor characteristic of a Bigarade Sauce; however, another variety of orange may be substituted.

Cooking squab in a cottage kitchen, c.1840.

SQUAB ON TOAST

6 squabs
2 tablespoons butter or
   margarine
2 slices bacon, diced
1 cup finely chopped onion
1 carrot, finely chopped
½ teaspoon salt
¾ cup sliced fresh
   mushrooms
⅓ cup Madeira or other dry
   sweet wine
6 slices bread, toasted

Remove giblets from squabs; reserve for other uses. Rinse squabs with cold water; pat dry.

Melt butter in a large skillet; add squabs, bacon, onion, carrot, and salt. Sauté until squabs are lightly browned on all sides and vegetable mixture is tender. Add mushrooms and wine; cover and simmer 45 minutes. Serve each squab on toasted bread; spoon sauce over squabs. Yield: 6 servings.

ROAST SQUAB PILAU

2 cups uncooked regular rice
4 cups chicken broth
6 slices bacon
¾ cup chopped celery
1 medium onion, chopped
4 eggs, beaten
1 teaspoon salt
⅛ teaspoon pepper
4 (14-ounce) squabs
¼ cup dry white wine

Combine rice and broth in a medium saucepan; bring to a boil. Reduce heat; cover and simmer 20 minutes or until rice is tender and broth is absorbed.

Cook bacon in a large skillet until crisp; remove bacon, reserving drippings in skillet. Crumble bacon, and set aside.

Sauté celery and onion in drippings until tender. Add bacon, celery, onion, eggs, salt, and pepper to cooked rice; stirring well.

Remove giblets and neck from squabs; reserve for other uses. Rinse squabs with cold water; pat dry. Stuff squabs with rice mixture (about ⅔ cup per squab).

Spoon remaining rice mixture into a lightly greased 13- x 9- x 2-inch baking dish. Place stuffed squabs on top of rice; cover lightly with foil. Bake at 400° for 30 minutes, basting every 10 minutes with wine. Remove foil, and bake an additional 10 minutes or until golden brown. Yield: 4 servings.

LOW COUNTRY ROAST SQUAB WITH RICE PILAU

4 squabs
3 tablespoons butter or
   margarine
1 medium onion, chopped
½ cup chopped celery
¼ cup chopped green pepper
3 (10¾-ounce) cans chicken
   broth, undiluted
1 cup uncooked regular rice
1 cup uncooked brown rice
4 eggs, beaten
½ teaspoon salt
⅛ teaspoon pepper

Remove giblets from squabs; reserve for other uses. Rinse squabs with cold water; pat dry.

Combine butter, onion, celery, and green pepper in a large skillet; sauté until vegetables are tender, and set aside.

Place chicken broth in a medium saucepan; bring to a boil. Stir in rice. Reduce heat; cover, and simmer 20 minutes or until rice is tender and broth is absorbed. Remove from heat. Add sautéed vegetables to the rice; stir well. Stir in remaining ingredients.

Stuff squabs with rice mixture (about ⅔ cup per squab). Place remaining rice mixture in a lightly greased 13- x 9- x 2-inch baking dish. Arrange stuffed squabs on top of rice mixture. Bake at 400° for 45 minutes. Yield: 4 servings.

For a special occasion: Roast Squab Pilau.

STUFFINGS AND GRAVIES

BREAD DRESSING

1 (1-pound) loaf bread, sliced
  and cubed
1 teaspoon poultry seasoning
¼ teaspoon pepper
¾ cup chopped onion
¾ cup chopped celery
1 cup butter or margarine

Combine bread, poultry seasoning, and pepper in a large bowl; set aside.

Sauté onion and celery in butter until tender; add to bread mixture, and stir well. Spoon into a lightly greased 1½-quart casserole. Bake, covered, at 325° for 20 minutes. Yield: about 6 servings.

ONION DRESSING PATTIES

1 large onion, chopped
1 cup chopped celery
3 tablespoons butter or
  margarine
2 cups cornbread crumbs
5 slices bread, toasted and
  crumbled (about 3¾ cups
  crumbs)
¼ teaspoon rubbed sage
⅛ teaspoon poultry seasoning
⅛ teaspoon ground thyme
2 hard-cooked eggs, chopped
1 egg
1 teaspoon Worcestershire
  sauce
½ cup chicken broth

Sauté onion and celery in butter until tender; stir in remaining ingredients, mixing well.

Shape stuffing into 9 patties; place on a lightly greased baking sheet. Bake at 350° for 20 minutes or until golden brown. Yield: 9 servings.

PEANUT DRESSING

2 cups dry roasted peanuts,
  finely ground
1½ cups toasted soft
  breadcrumbs
2 tablespoons butter or
  margarine, melted
½ teaspoon salt
¼ teaspoon pepper
1 egg yolk
½ cup chicken broth

Combine peanuts, breadcrumbs, butter, salt, and pepper, stirring lightly; add egg yolk and broth, mixing well.

Spoon dressing into a greased 1-quart casserole. Bake at 350° for 30 minutes or until lightly browned. Yield: 3 cups (or enough to stuff one 3-pound chicken).

POTATO STUFFING

4 cups cooked hot mashed
  potatoes
2 cups soft breadcrumbs
½ cup butter or margarine,
  melted
1 tablespoon plus 1 teaspoon
  onion juice
1 teaspoon salt
1 teaspoon rubbed sage
½ teaspoon pepper

Combine potatoes, breadcrumbs, butter, onion juice, salt, sage, and pepper, mixing well. Spoon mixture into a greased 1½-quart baking dish. Bake covered at 350° for 25 minutes. Uncover, and bake 5 minutes or until thoroughly heated. Yield: 4 cups (or enough to stuff one 3-pound duckling).

T empting and succulent as a plain roasted fowl can be, it may be further enhanced by the judicious application of savory stuffing (or dressing) and gravy. Southerners have inherited recipes for stuffings that, thanks to our superabundance of peanuts and pecans, are little used in other parts of the country.

But let's interrupt here to define our terms. We may as well say that stuffing and dressing are one and the same; stuffing is dressing cooked inside the bird. If that is agreeable with our fellow cooks, we can move on to the selection of embellishments for this bookful of birds.

The best guide to follow is your taste buds, and those of the people with whom you are to share your feast. If you know that sauerkraut wreaks havoc with your brother-in-law's digestion, and you value him, by all means select another stuffing for the goose.

Recipe writing, when it comes to dressing and gravy, can be an inexact science. The amount of liquid, for example, must be adjusted according to personal taste. Do you prefer a moist or crumbly dressing? A thick or thin gravy? Add the liquid gradually; then stop short if it appears to be too much for your liking. Or feel free to add more to get the consistency you prefer.

Our roast fowl gravy is based on a roux made from equal parts flour and the rich brown sediment of the pan drippings. If a browner gravy is your goal, either continue cooking the flour in the pan drippings until golden brown, or use flour which has been lightly browned in the oven.

WILD RICE DRESSING

½ cup wild rice, uncooked
3 cups water
½ pound fresh mushrooms, sliced
3 tablespoons butter or margarine
½ teaspoon rubbed sage
½ teaspoon salt
¼ teaspoon pepper
Dash ground thyme
1 egg yolk, beaten

Combine wild rice and water in a medium saucepan; bring to a boil. Reduce heat; cover and simmer 25 minutes. Set aside.

Sauté mushrooms in butter until tender. Add mushrooms, seasonings, and egg yolk to rice, stirring well. Spoon dressing into a lightly greased 1-quart casserole. Bake at 350° for 20 minutes or until thoroughly heated. Yield: 4 servings.

SAUERKRAUT STUFFING

4 cups chopped sauerkraut
2 cooking apples, cored and cut into ¼-inch slices
4 slices bacon, diced

Combine sauerkraut, apples, and bacon in a large Dutch oven; mix well. Cook over medium heat 20 minutes or until apples are tender.

Spoon stuffing into a lightly greased 1½-quart casserole. Bake at 350° for 20 minutes or until thoroughly heated. Yield: 8 cups (or enough to stuff one 11-pound turkey).

GIBLET GRAVY

Giblets and neck from 1 turkey or chicken
1 small onion, quartered
2 ribs of celery, halved
½ teaspoon salt
Pan drippings from 1 roasted turkey or chicken
3 tablespoons all-purpose flour

Combine giblets, except liver, neck, onion, celery, and salt in a small saucepan. (Set liver aside.) Cover with water; bring to a boil. Reduce heat; cover, and simmer 1 to 2 hours or until giblets are fork tender. Add liver, and simmer an additional 10 minutes. Drain, reserving giblet broth; discard onion and celery. Remove meat from neck; coarsely chop neck meat and giblets. Set aside.

Skim fat from pan drippings of roast turkey or chicken, being careful not to lose any of the brown sediment. Discard fat. Reserve pan drippings in roaster; add reserved giblet broth, stirring until sediment is loosened from bottom of roaster. Measure broth mixture and add water to equal 1½ cups, if necessary. Pour mixture into a medium-size saucepan.

Add flour to giblet broth mixture, stirring until smooth. Cook over medium heat, stirring constantly, until thickened and bubbly. Stir in reserved neck meat and giblets. Add salt and pepper to taste. Serve warm with roasted chicken or turkey and dressing, if desired. Yield: about 2 cups.

ROAST FOWL GRAVY

¼ cup pan drippings from 1 roasted turkey or chicken
¼ cup all-purpose flour
2 cups boiling water
½ teaspoon salt
¼ teaspoon pepper

Skim fat from pan drippings, being careful not to lose any of the brown sediment. Discard fat; leave ¼ cup pan drippings.

Pour pan drippings into a saucepan. Add flour, stirring until smooth. Cook over low heat 2 minutes, stirring constantly. Add water; cook over medium-high heat 1 minute, stirring constantly, until thickened and bubbly. Stir in salt and pepper. Yield: about 2 cups.

OYSTER SAUCE

1 tablespoon butter or margarine
1 tablespoon milk
3 tablespoons all-purpose flour
1 cup turkey or chicken broth
1 cup milk
1 (12-ounce) container fresh Select oysters, drained and chopped
1 tablespoon minced fresh parsley
½ teaspoon salt

Combine butter and 1 tablespoon milk in a heavy saucepan; cook over low heat, stirring constantly, until butter is melted. Add flour, stirring until smooth. Cook 1 minute, stirring constantly. Gradually add broth, 1 cup milk, and oysters; cook over medium heat, stirring constantly, until slightly thickened and bubbly. Stir in parsley and salt. Yield: about 3 cups.

A CHICKEN IN EVERY POT

Ancestral Pies, Puddings, and Such

J ust as a "chicken in every pot" has always been the poor man's dream, so has the chicken in too frequent a pot become the budget-minded cook's challenge. Of late years, chicken has been the bargain hunter's delight, making us scramble for different ways of presenting it. There is no reason for letting boredom come to the table with the bird, however, and that is the message of this chapter.

It is hoped, presupposed, in fact, that we all wash chicken before it is cooked. That's just in case the latest cookbook on your shelf is *The New Family Cookbook* by Juliet Corson. This 1885 epic was written from her position as Superintendent of the New York School of Cookery and no nonsense is in it. "In the preparation of poultry for cooking, it is not necessary to wash it unless it is in a very bad condition, and then it would be better not to use it...."

Miss Corson, it appears, was more of an evangelist than a cook when it came to food. She wrote numerous broadsides for the "working class," including one called "Twenty-Five Cent Dinners for Families of Six." How could a poor man afford chicken for Sunday dinner? "The chicken need not be tender, but it ought to be fleshy enough to furnish the basis for two meals." Let's be fair; if we could buy a five-pound hen for fifteen cents, surely for a dime we could eke out vegetables or dumplings enough for twelve servings all together? Long, slow stewing would be the ticket.

Back a little in history, Eliza Leslie came out with other advice in *Miss Leslie's New Cookery Book, 1857:* "Spring chickens bring a high price and are considered delicacies, but they are so insipid.... Wait till the young chickens grow into nice plump fowls...."

In 1824, years before either of the foregoing Yankee advice peddlers entered their careers, Mary Randolph wrote *The Virginia Housewife*, the first cookbook published in the South. Not only did she wash chickens, she found small ones quite to her liking for frying and fricasseeing.

For this chapter, though, the more mature the fowl, the better it is for our distinctive Southern dishes, as its well developed flavor will not be swamped by the other ingredients.

Camp Meeting-style Feast: At Felders Camp Ground in Mississippi, Grandmother's Chicken Pie takes top honors served with Southern-style green beans, old-time Onion Slaw, Candied Sweet Potatoes, garden tomatoes, feathery hot rolls, iced tea aplenty, and that glorious Egg Custard Pie.

CAMP MEETING FARE

What do you think of when someone mentions "camp meeting"? In frontier days, when people lived far apart, the advent of the traveling preacher was the occasion for farmers or ranchers to come to a central location, set up camp, greet old friends, and purge their souls with an old-fashioned religious revival. And, incidentally, to sink their teeth into all the good food the camp cooks could provide. In those times, it was customary for a few rowdy individuals to do some drinking and harmless firing of guns in the vicinity. Nobody paid them much attention. It was those rowdies, who sometimes "got religion."

In many Southern states even today, there are numerous camp grounds maintained by various denominations as religious retreats. One such camp was established in Pike County, Mississippi, in 1843. Originally Topisaw Camp Ground, it was renamed Felder's Camp Ground. Mrs. Helen Felder holds forth today as head cook, often serving chicken pie, a favorite of the campers.

GRANDMOTHER'S CHICKEN PIE
CANDIED SWEET POTATOES
GREEN BEANS WITH ONION SLAW
SLICED TOMATOES
HOMEMADE ROLLS
CHESS PIE * EGG CUSTARD PIE

Serves 6

Preparing for St. Thomas Church's picnic. Bardstown, Kentucky, 1940.

Emma Lee Moss committed memories to a painting called Church Picnic.

GRANDMOTHER'S CHICKEN PIE

3 whole chicken breasts, boned, skinned, and chopped
1 teaspoon salt
¼ teaspoon pepper
2 cups all-purpose flour
2 teaspoons baking powder
1 teaspoon salt
1 teaspoon sugar
½ teaspoon baking soda
¼ cup plus 2 tablespoons shortening
¾ cup buttermilk
½ cup butter or margarine
1½ cups hot water

Place chicken in a lightly greased 1½-quart casserole. Sprinkle with 1 teaspoon salt and pepper. Set aside.

Combine flour, baking powder, 1 teaspoon salt, sugar, and soda in a mixing bowl, stirring well. Cut in shortening with a pastry blender until mixture re-sembles coarse meal. Add buttermilk, stirring until dry ingredients are moistened.

Turn dough out on a floured surface, and knead lightly 4 or 5 times. Roll dough to ¼-inch thickness; cut into 1-inch strips.

Cover chicken with strips of dough, and dot with butter. Pour hot water evenly over top of pie. Bake, covered, at 300° for 1½ hours. Remove cover, and bake an additional 20 minutes or until crust is golden brown. Yield: 6 servings.

CANDIED SWEET POTATOES

3 large sweet potatoes
1 cup firmly packed brown sugar
½ cup sugar
1 tablespoon all-purpose flour
1 teaspoon salt
1 cup water
1½ tablespoons butter or margarine, melted
1 tablespoon corn syrup
1 teaspoon vanilla extract

Cook sweet potatoes in boiling water 30 minutes or until tender. Let cool to touch; peel and cut into ½-inch slices. Arrange slices in a lightly greased 13- x 9- x 2-inch baking dish.

Combine sugar, flour, and salt in a medium saucepan. Add remaining ingredients, stirring well; bring to a boil. Remove from heat, and pour syrup over sweet potatoes. Bake at 325° for 2 hours. Yield: 6 servings.

53

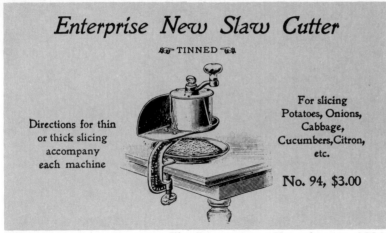

Enterprise New Slaw Cutter

◆═ TINNED ═◆

Directions for thin
or thick slicing
accompany
each machine

For slicing
Potatoes, Onions,
Cabbage,
Cucumbers, Citron,
etc.

No. 94, $3.00

Slaw cutter advertisement: The Enterprising Housekeeper, *1898.*

GREEN BEANS WITH ONION SLAW

2 pounds fresh green beans
2 tablespoons bacon
    drippings
1 teaspoon sugar
1½ teaspoons salt
¼ teaspoon pepper
4 cups water
Onion Slaw

Remove strings from beans; wash and cut into 1½-inch pieces. Combine beans, drippings, sugar, salt, pepper, and water in a large Dutch oven; bring to a boil. Reduce heat; cover and simmer 2 hours or until beans are tender. Serve Onion Slaw over beans. Yield: 6 servings.

Onion Slaw:

3 medium onions, chopped
1 cup plus 2 tablespoons
    vinegar
1½ teaspoons sugar
½ teaspoon salt
¼ teaspoon pepper

Combine all ingredients in a medium bowl; stir well. Cover, and chill at least 1 hour before serving. Yield: about 1½ cups.

HOMEMADE ROLLS

¼ cup plus 2 tablespoons
    shortening
¼ cup sugar
¾ teaspoon salt
½ cup boiling water
1 package dry yeast
½ cup warm water (105° to
    115°)
3 cups all-purpose flour,
    divided
1 egg, slightly beaten

Combine shortening, sugar, and salt in a large mixing bowl. Pour boiling water over shortening mixture, stirring until shortening melts and sugar dissolves. Cool to 105° to 115°.

Dissolve yeast in warm water; stir well. Let stand 5 minutes.

Add 1 cup flour to shortening mixture; stir well. Add yeast mixture, egg, and remaining flour, stirring until blended.

Turn dough out on a floured surface, and knead 3 or 4 times. Place in a greased bowl, turning to grease top. Cover and let rise in a warm place (85°), free from drafts, 55 minutes or until doubled in bulk.

Punch dough down, and shape into 1-inch balls. Place ½ inch apart in a greased 13- x 9- x 2-inch baking pan. Cover and let rise in a warm place (85°), free from drafts, 1 hour or until doubled in bulk. Bake at 400° for 10 to 15 minutes. Yield: 2 dozen.

CHESS PIE

5 eggs
2 cups sugar
1 tablespoon cornmeal
¼ cup plus 2 tablespoons
    butter or margarine, melted
2 tablesoons lemon juice
1½ teaspoons vanilla extract
Pastry (recipe follows)

Beat eggs with a wire whisk or fork; add next 3 ingredients, mixing well. Stir in lemon juice and vanilla; pour into prepared pastry shell. Bake at 400° for 10 minutes. Reduce heat to 350°, and bake an additional 30 minutes. Yield: one 9-inch pie.

Pastry:

1⅓ cups all-purpose flour
½ teaspoon salt
⅛ teaspoon ground nutmeg
⅓ cup vegetable oil
3 tablespoons cold milk

Combine flour, salt, and nutmeg; add oil and milk, stirring until mixture forms a ball.

Roll dough to ⅛-inch thickness on a lightly floured surface. Fit pastry into a 9-inch pieplate. Yield: one 9-inch pastry shell.

EGG CUSTARD PIE

3 eggs, slighty beaten
1 cup sugar
2 tablespoons butter or
    margarine, melted
1½ teaspoons vanilla extract
2 cups milk
1 unbaked 9-inch pastry shell

Combine eggs, sugar, butter, and vanilla; beat until blended. Stir in milk, and pour into pastry shell.

Bake at 350° for 45 minutes or until a knife inserted 1 inch from edge of pie comes out clean. Cool 10 minutes. Yield: one 9-inch pie.

IN THE ENGLISH TRADITION

REAL CHICKEN PIE

1 (6- to 6½-pound) baking
   hen, cut up
2 stalks celery, chopped
¼ cup chopped onion
2 tablespoons chopped fresh
   parsley
¼ cup plus 2 tablespoons
   all-purpose flour
1 cup milk
1 teaspoon salt
½ teaspoon pepper
Pastry for 10-inch
   double-crust pie

Combine chicken, celery, onion, and parsley in a large Dutch oven; add water to cover.

Cook, covered, 2 hours or until chicken is tender. Remove chicken from broth; cool. Remove meat from bones, and chop into bite-size pieces; set aside. Strain broth, and discard vegetables. Refrigerate chicken broth until all fat has risen to the top; skim off 6 tablespoons fat, and set aside. Discard excess fat, reserving 2 cups broth.

Melt reserved fat in a heavy saucepan over low heat; add flour, stirring until smooth. Cook 1 minute, stirring constantly. Gradually add milk and reserved broth; cook over medium heat, stirring constantly, until thickened and bubbly. Stir in salt, pepper, and chopped chicken.

Roll two-thirds of pastry to ⅛-inch thickness on a lightly floured surface; fit into a 2-quart casserole. Spoon chicken mixture into pastry shell.

Roll out remaining pastry to ⅛-inch thickness; carefully place over chicken mixture, leaving a 1-inch overhang at edge of casserole dish. Turn pastry edges under; press firmly to rim of casserole to seal and flute. Cut slits in top. Bake at 425° for 40 minutes or until golden brown. If pastry gets too brown, cover lightly with aluminum foil. Yield: 8 servings.

Chickens don't have to be called twice when it's feeding time.

Valentine Museum, Richmond, Virginia

55

A real Southern treat: Chicken Pie with Sweet Potato Crust.

CHICKEN PIE WITH SWEET POTATO CRUST

3 cups cubed cooked chicken
1 cup diced cooked carrots
6 pearl onions, cooked
1 tablespoon chopped fresh parsley
2 tablespoons all-purpose flour
1 teaspoon salt
⅛ teaspoon pepper
1 cup evaporated milk
1 cup chicken broth
Sweet Potato Crust

Combine first 4 ingredients; spoon into a 10- x 6- x 2-inch baking dish.

Combine flour, salt, and pepper in a heavy saucepan. Gradually stir in milk and broth. Cook over medium heat, stirring constantly, until thickened and bubbly. Pour sauce over chicken-vegetable mixture; top with Sweet Potato Crust. Turn pastry edges under; press firmly to rim of casserole to seal, and flute. (Make decorative design with excess pastry.) Cut slits in crust to allow steam to escape. Bake at 350° for 40 minutes or until crust is lightly browned. Yield: 6 servings.

Sweet Potato Crust:

1 cup all-purpose flour
1 teaspoon baking powder
½ teaspoon salt
1 cup cooked, mashed sweet potatoes
⅓ cup butter or margarine, melted
1 egg, beaten

Combine flour, baking powder, and salt. Stir in remaining ingredients, blending well. Refrigerate dough at least 2 hours. Turn dough out onto a lightly floured surface. Roll to ¼-inch thickness; trim to ½ inch larger than casserole. Yield: pastry for one 10- x 6- x 2-inch pie.

GOLDEN CHICKEN POT PIE

1 cup chopped carrots
1 cup chopped onion
1 cup fresh or frozen English peas
½ cup chopped celery
3 cups chopped cooked chicken
1 tablespoon chopped fresh parsley
¼ cup plus 2 tablespoons butter or margarine
¼ cup plus 2 tablespoons all-purpose flour
2 cups chicken broth
1 cup half-and-half
1 teaspoon salt
¼ teaspoon pepper
Sweet Potato Crust (see left)

Combine first 4 ingredients in a medium saucepan; add water to cover. Bring to a boil. Cover; reduce heat, and simmer 20 minutes or until vegetables are tender. Drain.

Combine cooked vegetables, chicken, and parsley in a shallow 2½-quart casserole. Set mixture aside.

Melt butter in a heavy saucepan; blend in flour. Cook over low heat until bubbly, stirring constantly. Gradually add broth and half-and-half; cook, stirring constantly, until thickened and bubbly. Stir in salt and pepper. Pour over vegetables and chicken in casserole.

Top with Sweet Potato Crust. Turn pastry edges under, and press firmly to rim of casserole to seal. Cut slits in top of pastry. Bake at 350° for 40 minutes or until pastry is browned. Yield: 6 to 8 servings.

Note: Use excess pastry for decorative design.

PIGEON PIE

Chicken pie, pigeon pie...if they remind you of "four and twenty blackbirds," you'll be right on track. Meat pies and puddings are strictly English in origin. Cornish "pasties" were carried for lunch by miners in Cornwall centuries ago and are still served as pick-up food in British pubs. The crust is a container encasing meat, vegetables, and gravy.

About those blackbirds: As in so many of the old English bits and pieces we have memorized, there is truth behind the seemingly silly verse. Aviaries were commercial enterprises in Europe from Medieval days into the 1600s. Those who could afford them ate ortolans (now rare), thrushes, and all kinds of songbirds.

In reality, the blackbird number was among the lesser conceits that figured in party entertainments in certain circles. By paraphrasing some research, we can tell you how to make such a "pye" for your next important occasion. It would make a fine surprise for, say, a spouse's birthday:

First, forget flaky and tender; think tough. Make a strong dough of flour, lard, and water. Roll it out thickly and use it to line a deep pan; that is the "coffin." Fill the pan level full with "flower." Cover with pastry and bake. Turn the pye out, cut a hole in the bottom, shake out the flower, and put in ye blackbirds. Place a serving dish over it, working quickly, and invert. Place it before the guest of honor, and when the pye is opened, well, just think of the fun!

4 squabs
½ teaspoon celery salt
¼ teaspoon paprika
2 dozen medium-size fresh mushrooms, sliced
2 hard-cooked eggs, chopped
¾ teaspoon pepper, divided
3 tablespoons all-purpose flour
1 cup milk
½ teaspoon salt
Pastry (recipe follows)

Remove giblets from squabs; set aside. Combine squabs, celery salt, and paprika in a large Dutch oven; add water to cover. Simmer 1 hour or until squabs are tender. Add reserved giblets during last 20 minutes of cooking time.

Remove squabs and giblets from broth; reserve 2 cups broth in Dutch oven. Chop giblets. Remove meat from bones, and chop. Spoon half of chopped squabs into a greased 2-quart casserole. Spread half of chopped giblets, mushrooms, and eggs over top. Sprinkle with ¼ teaspoon pepper. Repeat procedure with remaining squab, giblets, mushrooms, eggs, and ¼ teaspoon pepper.

Combine flour and milk; stir until smooth. Pour flour mixture into reserved 2 cups broth; cook, stirring constantly, until thickened and bubbly. Stir in remaining pepper and salt. Pour gravy over layered mixture in casserole.

Prepare pastry. Roll dough to ½-inch thickness; place over pie leaving a ½-inch overhang at edge of dish. Turn pastry edges under; press firmly to rim of casserole to seal, and flute. Cut slits in top for steam to escape. Bake at 400° for 25 minutes or until crust is lightly browned. Yield: 6 servings.

Pastry:

2 cups all-purpose flour
1 tablespoon baking powder
½ teaspoon salt
⅓ cup shortening
¾ cup milk

Combine flour, baking powder, and salt; stir well. Cut in shortening with a pastry blender until mixture resembles coarse meal. Sprinkle milk over flour mixture, stirring until dry ingredients are moistened. Turn dough out onto a lightly floured surface; knead lightly 4 to 5 times. Roll pastry to fit casserole. Yield: enough pastry for 2-quart casserole.

Passenger pigeons, represented by painter Walter Thorp.

University of Wisconsin

Maryland Chicken Pudding, a recipe so old that it's new again.

VIRGINIA CHICKEN PUDDING

1 (3- to 3½-pound)
　broiler-fryer, cut up
1 medium onion, halved
1 stalk celery, sliced
3 sprigs fresh parsley
2½ teaspoons salt, divided
½ teaspoon ground thyme
½ teaspoon pepper, divided
1¾ cups all-purpose flour,
　divided
⅓ cup plus 2 tablespoons
　butter or margarine, melted
　and divided
3 eggs
1 cup milk
¾ cup plus 2 tablespoons
　water, divided
1 tablespoon all-purpose flour

Combine chicken giblets, neck, and backbone with onion, celery, parsley, 1 teaspoon salt, thyme, and ¼ teaspoon pepper in a medium saucepan; add water to cover. Bring to a boil; cover and simmer 45 minutes. Strain and reserve broth. Discard meat and vegetables.

Combine ½ cup flour, 1 teaspoon salt, and remaining ¼ teaspoon pepper. Dredge chicken pieces in flour mixture, coating well; brown in ⅓ cup butter in a large skillet over medium heat. Add reserved broth to chicken. Bring to a boil; cover and simmer 45 minutes or until chicken is tender. Remove chicken from skillet, and cool; reserve broth. Remove meat from bone; dice, and place in a 1½-quart casserole.

Combine eggs, milk, and 2 tablespoons butter; beat well. Add 1¼ cups flour and ½ teaspoon salt; beat well. Pour batter over chicken; bake at 450° for 15 minutes. Reduce temperature to 350°; bake 20 minutes or until lightly browned.

Stir ¾ cup water into reserved chicken broth. Combine 1 tablespoon flour and remaining water, mixing well; stir into chicken broth. Cook mixture over medium-high heat, stirring constantly, until thickened and bubbly. Serve gravy with pudding. Yield: 4 to 6 servings.

MARYLAND CHICKEN PUDDING

1 (3½- to 4-pound)
　broiler-fryer, cut up
1 medium onion, sliced
3 fresh celery leaves
3 sprigs fresh parsley
½ teaspoon ground thyme
½ teaspoon dried whole
　rosemary
2 teaspoons salt, divided
½ teaspoon pepper, divided
3 eggs, beaten
2 cups milk
1½ cups all-purpose flour,
　divided
¼ cup plus 2 tablespoons
　butter or margarine, melted
　and divided
3 tablespoons chopped fresh
　parsley

Combine first 6 ingredients, 1 teaspoon salt, and ¼ teaspoon pepper in a Dutch oven; add water to cover. Bring to a boil; cover and simmer 1½ hours. Remove chicken from broth; cool. Strain broth, and set aside.

Remove chicken meat from bone; dice and place in a 10-inch cast-iron skillet. Pour ½ cup broth over chicken. Set remaining broth aside.

Combine eggs, milk, 1 cup flour, ½ teaspoon salt, and ¼ cup butter; beat until smooth. Pour over chicken in skillet. Bake at 375° for 1 hour. Cool and cut into wedges.

Cook remaining broth over high heat until reduced to 2 cups. Stir in ½ cup flour. Add parsley, 2 tablespoons butter, ½ teaspoon salt, and ¼ teaspoon pepper. Cook over medium heat until thickened and bubbly. Spoon gravy over pudding. Yield: 8 servings.

MARY RANDOLPH'S CHICKEN PUDDING

2 (3- to 3½-pound) broiler-fryers, cut up
3 sprigs fresh parsley
2 stalks celery with leaves, halved
1 small onion, sliced
2 teaspoons salt
½ teaspoon whole peppercorns
½ teaspoon dried whole thyme
3½ quarts water
5 eggs
2 cups milk
¼ cup butter or margarine, melted
2½ cups all-purpose flour, divided
1½ teaspoons salt, divided
¼ teaspoon pepper
⅛ teaspoon paprika

Combine first 8 ingredients in a large Dutch oven; cover and simmer 1 hour or until chicken is tender.

Remove chicken from broth; let cool. Bone chicken; cut into bite-size pieces, and arrange in a 13- x 9- x 2-inch baking dish. Strain ¼ cup broth, and pour over chicken; set aside. Reserve remaining broth.

Beat eggs until frothy; gradually add milk and butter, beating well. Add 2 cups flour and ½ teaspoon salt, mixing well. Pour egg mixture over chicken. Bake at 350° for 40 minutes or until pudding is set.

Simmer reserved broth, uncovered, for 40 minutes while pudding is baking. Remove broth from heat; strain. Pour 3 cups broth in a small saucepan. Blend remaining ½ cup flour with a small amount of water, mixing to form a smooth paste; stir into broth. Cook over medium heat, stirring constantly, until thickened and bubbly. Stir in remaining salt, pepper, and paprika.

Cut chicken pudding into squares, and serve with gravy. Yield: 8 servings.

Symphony Chicken loaf for an elegant little dinner.

SYMPHONY CHICKEN LOAF

2⅔ cups chicken broth
1¾ cups herb-seasoned stuffing mix
3½ cups cubed cooked chicken
1½ cups cooked rice
4 eggs, beaten
¼ cup finely chopped green pepper
¼ cup chopped pimiento
½ teaspoon salt
Mushroom Sauce
Green pepper rings (optional)
Pimiento strips (optional)

Pour chicken broth over stuffing mix; let stand 10 minutes.

Combine chicken, rice, eggs, chopped green pepper, chopped pimiento, and salt, stirring well. Add chicken mixture to stuffing mixture, stirring until blended. Spoon mixture into a heavily greased 9- x 5- x 3-inch loaf pan. Place in a shallow pan containing about 1 inch water. Bake at 350° for 1 hour. Cool completely before inverting onto a serving platter. Serve with Mushroom Sauce. Garnish with green pepper rings and pimiento strips, if desired. Yield: 8 servings.

Mushroom Sauce:

¼ cup plus 2 tablespoons butter or margarine
¼ cup plus 2 tablespoons all-purpose flour
3 cups chicken broth
½ cup half-and-half
1½ cups sliced fresh mushrooms
2 tablespoons chopped fresh parsley
1 teaspoon lemon juice
½ teaspoon paprika

Melt butter in a heavy saucepan over low heat; gradually add flour, stirring until smooth. Cook 1 minute, stirring constantly. Gradually add broth; cook over medium heat, stirring constantly, until thickened and bubbly. Remove from heat, and stir in remaining ingredients. Yield: 4 cups.

KETTLE COOKERY

HOPKINS COUNTY STEW

1 (6- to 6½-pound) baking
   hen, cut up
¼ cup butter or margarine,
   melted
4 cups diced potatoes
2 medium onions, chopped
4 cups chicken broth
1 (28-ounce) can whole
   tomatoes, undrained and
   finely chopped
1 teaspoon sugar
1 teaspoon chili powder
1 teaspoon paprika
1 teaspoon salt
½ teaspoon pepper
1 (17-ounce) can cream-style
   corn

Brown chicken in butter in a
large skillet; remove chicken,
and set aside to cool. Bone
chicken, and cut meat into 2-
inch pieces.

Place potatoes and onion in a
large Dutch oven. Add broth;
stir well. Cover and cook 1 hour
or until vegetables are tender.
Add tomatoes; continue cooking, covered, 20 minutes. Add
chicken, sugar, and seasonings;
stir well. Cook, covered, over low
heat 3 hours, stirring occasionally. Stir in corn; cook an additional 30 minutes. Yield: 4½
quarts or 12 to 15 servings.

Collection of Business Americana

KENTUCKY BURGOO

1 (3- to 3½-pound)
   broiler-fryer, cut up
2 pounds beef shank
½ pound veal
4 quarts water
1 tablespoon salt
1 teaspoon pepper
⅛ teaspoon red pepper
2 cups peeled, cubed potatoes
2 cups chopped onion
2 cups sliced fresh okra
1 cup chopped carrots
1 cup chopped fresh parsley
2 (17-ounce) cans whole
   kernel corn, undrained
1 (28-ounce) can whole
   tomatoes, undrained and
   chopped
1 (10-ounce) package frozen
   baby lima beans
2 medium-size green peppers,
   chopped
1 clove garlic, minced

Combine chicken, beef
shank, veal, water, and seasonings in an 8½-quart stock pot.
Bring to a boil; cover and simmer 2 hours. Remove chicken,
beef, and veal from broth. Remove meat from bones, and cut
into pieces. Return meat to
broth, stirring well.

Add remaining ingredients.
Simmer, uncovered, 2 hours,
stirring frequently. Yield: 6
quarts or 24 servings.

*Kentucky Burgoo: time-
consuming but worth it!*

The legendary Gus Jaubert's name lives in Kentucky
because he made a career of burgoo. Gus "trailed"
with his 600-gallon iron kettle, and the late Tandy
Ellis, a newspaper columnist, learned burgoo from him. Ellis
played that recipe close to his chest until a food writer published a burgoo with cabbage in it. That brought out the
fight in Ellis, causing him to divulge "the right way to make
burgoo."

In Hopkins County, Texas, a week-long fall festival culmi-
nates in the Annual World Championship Stew Cookoff.
Variations may contain "bear, beef, chicken, rabbit, or
squirrel." Except for the chili powder in it, the namesake recipe could pass for burgoo; both mixtures are cooked until the
corn kernels are the only recognizable food.

Anyone possessed of an iron kettle and a basic dressed hen is in a position to spend a day making chicken gumbo, stew, soup, or burgoo. You may even use some other container and add other meats; just don't forget the chicken. One of the most delicious ways to spend a day and a chicken is with gumbo. Gumbo comes in flavors other than chicken, but always includes okra or filé powder, or both, as a thickening agent.

CHICKEN GUMBO

1 (4- to 5-pound) baking hen, cut up
½ cup salt pork drippings
2 large onions, chopped
1 medium-size green pepper, chopped
4 cups sliced okra
1 cup chopped celery
¼ cup chopped fresh parsley
2 quarts water
8 medium tomatoes, peeled and quartered
1 tablespoon salt
½ teaspoon pepper
Hot cooked rice
Filé powder (optional)

Brown chicken in drippings in a large Dutch oven. Remove chicken, and set aside. Reserve drippings in Dutch oven.

Add onion, green pepper, okra, celery, and parsley to Dutch oven; cook over low heat 30 minutes, stirring frequently. Return chicken to Dutch oven.

Add water, tomatoes, salt, and pepper, stirring well. Simmer, uncovered, 2½ hours or until chicken is tender. Remove chicken from gumbo; bone and chop meat. Return meat to gumbo, stirring well. Cook until thoroughly heated.

Serve gumbo over rice. Add a small amount of filé powder to each serving, if desired. Yield: 1½ quarts or 4 to 6 servings.

CHICKEN AND OYSTER GUMBO

1 (3½- to 4-pound) broiler-fryer, cut up and skinned
⅓ cup shortening
½ cup all-purpose flour
1 large onion, chopped
3 quarts water
1 to 1½ teaspoons salt
¼ teaspoon pepper
⅛ teaspoon red pepper
½ cup chopped green onion tops
⅓ cup chopped fresh parsley
3 (12-ounce) containers fresh Select oysters, drained
2 teaspoons filé powder, (optional)
Hot cooked rice

Brown chicken in hot shortening in a large Dutch oven. Remove from Dutch oven; drain well, reserving shortening in Dutch oven.

Add flour to hot shortening; cook over medium heat, stirring constantly, 10 minutes or until roux is the color of a copper penny. Add chopped onion; cover, and cook 10 minutes.

Gradually add water to roux, stirring until well blended. Stir in chicken, salt, and pepper. Simmer, uncovered, 1½ hours, stirring occasionally.

Add green onion tops and parsley; simmer 10 minutes. Stir in oysters, and simmer an additional 5 minutes. Remove from heat; stir in filé powder to thicken gumbo, if desired. Serve gumbo over rice. Yield: 2½ quarts or 8 to 10 servings.

SAVANNAH CHICKEN GUMBO

1 (3- to 3½-pound) broiler-fryer, cut up
½ cup butter or margarine, divided
3 quarts water
3 tablespoons all-purpose flour
2 (17-ounce) cans whole kernel corn, undrained
2 (14½-ounce) cans whole tomatoes, undrained and finely chopped
4 cups sliced okra
1 (10-ounce) package frozen baby lima beans
1 tablespoon chopped fresh parsley
1 teaspoon sugar
1 teaspoon salt
½ teaspoon pepper
½ teaspoon crushed red pepper

Brown chicken in ¼ cup butter in a large Dutch oven. Add water, and simmer 1 hour or until chicken is tender. Remove chicken from broth and set broth aside. Remove meat from bones; cut into 2-inch pieces, and set aside.

Melt remaining butter in Dutch oven; stir in flour. Cook over medium heat, stirring occasionally, 10 minutes or until roux is the color of a copper penny. Stir in remaining ingredients; simmer for 10 minutes. Add chicken and reserved broth; cook over low heat 30 minutes or until vegetables are tender. Yield: 4½ quarts or 12 to 15 servings.

Vendors and early morning shoppers gather in New Orleans' French Market in this sketch by Alfred R. Waud, 1871.

EASY CHICKEN GUMBO

2 (3-pound) broiler-fryers, cut up
1 quart water
1 stalk celery, chopped
1 teaspoon salt
½ teaspoon pepper
1 (14½-ounce) can whole tomatoes, undrained
1 (10-ounce) package frozen cut okra
½ cup chopped celery
½ cup chopped onion
½ cup finely shredded cabbage

Combine chicken, water, chopped celery stalk, salt, and pepper in a large Dutch oven. Bring to a boil; cover and simmer 1 hour or until chicken is tender. Remove chicken from broth; cool. Bone chicken, and cut into 1-inch cubes. Strain broth, and return broth to Dutch oven. Discard celery.

Add next 4 ingredients to broth; cook over low heat 15 minutes. Add cabbage; cook an additional 5 minutes. Stir in chicken, and bring mixture to a boil. Serve immediately. Yield: 1½ quarts or 4 to 6 servings.

DUCK GUMBO

1 (4- to 4½-pound) dressed duckling
10 cups water
8 stalks celery, halved
3 bay leaves
1 large onion, sliced
1 teaspoon pepper
2 (10-ounce) packages frozen cut okra
1 tablespoon shortening
6 green onions, chopped
About 4 cups hot cooked rice
Chopped chives

Remove giblets from duckling. Combine giblets, duckling, water, celery, bay leaves, onion, and pepper in a large Dutch oven; bring to a boil. Reduce heat to low, and simmer 1 hour or until meat and vegetables are tender.

Remove duckling from broth; cool. Remove meat from bones; chop meat, and set aside. Strain broth, reserving broth in Dutch oven. Chop giblets finely, and set aside. Discard vegetables and bay leaves.

Sauté okra in hot shortening in a large skillet 10 minutes. Add green onion and chopped duckling; sauté an additional 5 minutes. Add to reserved broth, and simmer 1 hour.

Combine chopped giblets and rice. Serve gumbo over rice mixture, and sprinkle with chives. Yield: about 1½ quarts or 4 to 6 servings.

Brunswick Stew is brewing in the iron kettle
on the fire, the cook intent upon keeping it from sticking.
The guests (or is it the hosts?) stand by.

BRUNSWICK STEW

1 (3- to 3½-pound)
  broiler-fryer, cut up
1½ teaspoons salt
¼ teaspoon pepper
3 small onions, sliced
2 tablespoons bacon
  drippings
3 cups water
3 tomatoes, peeled and
  quartered
½ cup sherry
2 teaspoons Worcestershire
  sauce
1 (16-ounce) package frozen
  lima beans
3 ears fresh corn kernels, cut
  from cob
1 (10-ounce) package frozen
  cut okra

Sprinkle chicken with salt
and pepper. Set aside.

Sauté onion in drippings in a
large Dutch oven. Add chicken,
and brown on all sides. Add
water, tomatoes, sherry, and
Worcestershire sauce. Bring to a
boil; cover and simmer 30 minutes. Remove chicken from liquid, and cool. Bone chicken,
and cut meat into 2-inch pieces.
Return chicken to liquid. Add
vegetables. Simmer, uncovered,
1 hour, stirring occasionally.
Yield: about 2½ quarts or 6 to 8
servings.

Brunswick stew comes
either from Bruns-
wick, Georgia, or
Brunswick, Virginia; that
jury is still out. We do know
it goes back to the settlers'
early kettle cookery, starting
as soon as there were vegetables to throw into the pot
with the day's rabbit or
squirrel.

Chicken for Dinner, *painted by Clara McDonald Williamson.*

FARMER'S CHICKEN STEW

1 (2½- to 3-pound) broiler-fryer, cut and skinned
1 small cabbage, finely shredded
12 large tomatoes, peeled and sliced
2 medium onions, chopped
4 large potatoes, peeled and cubed
3 cups frozen cut okra
2 (17-ounce) cans whole kernel corn, undrained
3 quarts water
1 tablespoon salt
½ teaspoon pepper
⅛ teaspoon red pepper

Combine chicken with remaining ingredients in a large Dutch oven, stirring well; cover and simmer 1 hour.

Remove soup mixture from heat; set aside. Remove chicken from mixture; cool. Remove chicken from bones; chop meat into bite-size pieces.

Return chopped chicken to soup mixture. Heat thoroughly, stirring occasionally, before serving. Yield: 5 quarts or 15 to 18 servings.

FRESH VEGETABLE AND CHICKEN STEW

3 tablespoons shortening
1 (3- to 3½-pound) broiler-fryer, cut up
6½ cups water, divided
5 medium onions, chopped
1 cup diced potatoes
1 cup sliced carrots
1 cup frozen lima beans
2 teaspoons salt
½ to ¾ teaspoon pepper
⅓ cup all-purpose flour

Melt shortening in a large Dutch oven. Sauté chicken in shortening until brown on all sides. Add 6 cups water, and bring to a boil. Cover and simmer 1 hour or until chicken is tender. Remove chicken from broth; cool. Bone chicken, and chop meat.

Bring broth to a boil; stir in chopped chicken, onion, potatoes, carrots, lima beans, salt, and pepper; simmer, uncovered, 30 minutes.

Combine flour and remaining water, stirring until smooth. Stir flour mixture into stew; cook, stirring constantly, until thickened. Yield: about 2 quarts or 6 to 8 servings.

TURKEY CHOWDER

1 large onion, thinly sliced
2 stalks celery, sliced
¼ cup plus 1 tablespoon butter or margarine
¼ cup plus 1 tablespoon all-purpose flour
1 teaspoon salt
¼ teaspoon pepper
5½ cups turkey or chicken broth
2 medium potatoes, peeled and cubed
2 medium carrots, scraped and sliced
2 medium zucchini, cubed
1 (10-ounce) package frozen whole kernel corn
2 cups chopped turkey
½ cup dry white wine
2 tablespoons chopped fresh parsley

Sauté onion and celery in butter in a large Dutch oven until tender. Remove from heat; blend in flour, salt, and pepper. Gradually stir in broth; bring to a boil. Add potatoes and carrots; cover and simmer 15 minutes. Add next 4 ingredients; simmer 25 to 30 minutes, stirring occasionally. Stir in parsley. Yield: 4½ quarts or 12 to 15 servings.

ONE-DISH DELIGHTS

HEARTY ARROZ CON POLLO

½ cup all-purpose flour
1 (3½- to 4-pound) broiler-fryer, cut up
½ cup vegetable oil
1 large onion, chopped
7 brown-and-serve sausage links, cut into ½-inch slices
1 (28-ounce) can whole tomatoes, undrained
2 (4-ounce) jars chopped pimiento, drained
1 (3-ounce) jar pimiento-stuffed olives, drained
2 cups uncooked regular rice
1 cup water
2 chicken bouillon cubes
1½ teaspoons salt
¼ teaspoon pepper
1 (10-ounce) package frozen English peas

Place flour in a plastic or paper bag; add 2 or 3 pieces of chicken to bag, and shake well. Repeat procedure with remaining chicken. Heat oil in a Dutch oven; add chicken, and brown on all sides. Remove chicken, reserving oil in Dutch oven. Drain chicken on paper towels.

Sauté onion in reserved oil until tender. Add next 9 ingredients, stirring well. Place chicken pieces on top; cover and cook over medium heat 30 minutes. Stir mixture occasionally to prevent rice from sticking.

Stir in peas. Continue cooking, uncovered, 10 minutes. Yield: 4 to 6 servings.

CHICKEN AND YELLOW RICE

2 (3- to 3½-pound) broiler-fryers, cut up and skinned
1 cup olive oil
2 large onions, chopped
1 medium-size green pepper, chopped
4 cloves garlic, minced
1½ quarts water
2 cups uncooked regular rice
1 (15-ounce) can tomato sauce
1½ teaspoons salt
½ teaspoon ground saffron
¼ teaspoon pepper
1 bay leaf
1 (8½-ounce) can English peas, drained
1 (8-ounce) can sliced mushrooms, drained
1 (4-ounce) jar chopped pimiento, drained

Brown chicken in oil on all sides in a large ovenproof Dutch oven. Remove chicken, and set aside; reserve oil in Dutch oven. Sauté onion, green pepper, and garlic in oil. Stir in next 7 ingredients, and bring mixture to a boil.

Add chicken, stirring gently; cover and bake at 350° for 20 minutes or until rice is tender. Add peas, mushrooms, and pimiento; stir gently. Cover and bake an additional 10 minutes or until thoroughly heated. Remove bay leaf, and serve immediately. Yield: 8 to 10 servings.

Old-time Texas rice threshing scene

Paella Valenciana: Olé!

PAELLA VALENCIANA

¾ cup olive oil
1 (2½- to 3-pound)
   broiler-fryer, cut up
1 pound boneless pork, cut
   into 1-inch cubes
3 cloves garlic, crushed
½ pound red snapper, cut
   into 2-inch pieces
½ pound medium shrimp,
   peeled and deveined
½ pound fresh crabmeat,
   drained and flaked
4 ounces fresh small
   scallops
4 ounces fresh Select
   oysters, drained
1 medium onion, chopped
1 medium-size green pepper,
   chopped
1 quart chicken broth
1 small tomato, peeled and
   chopped

2½ cups uncooked regular
   rice
2 bay leaves
Dash of ground saffron
1 drop yellow food coloring
1 tablespoon salt
¼ teaspoon pepper
1 (10-ounce) package frozen
   English peas
1 (4-ounce) jar whole
   pimiento, drained and cut
   into strips
½ cup Chablis or other dry
   white wine
Lemon wedges (optional)

Heat oil in an 8½-quart oven-proof Dutch oven. Add chicken, pork, and garlic; cook until chicken and pork are browned on all sides. Add red snapper, shrimp, crabmeat, scallops, oys-ters, onion, and green pepper; cover and cook over medium heat 20 minutes or until snap-per is fork tender. Add broth, to-mato, and rice; bring mixture to a boil. Stir in bay leaves, saf-fron, food coloring, salt, and pepper; reduce heat, and cook over medium heat 10 minutes, stirring occasionally. Cover and bake at 350° for 15 minutes. Re-move bay leaf.

Cook peas according to pack-age directions; stir in pimiento. Spoon paella in center of platter and surround with peas. Sprin-kle wine over paella; garnish with lemon wedges, if desired. Yield: 8 to 10 servings.

Note: ¼ teaspoon ground saf-fron may be added for more fla-vor and color.

Jambalaya stems from the French jambon, meaning ham. The fame of this heady olio of ham, chicken, and rice from New Orleans has spread far from home just as has another gift from the French Creoles: pilaf. Pilaf (or pilaff or pilau) is now a staple food in the rice-growing, rice-eating states of the South. The rice must remain fluffy, never mushy; the consistency moist, never dry. However the word is spelled, the dish is somehow at its most charming when pronounced "perloo."

HAM AND CHICKEN JAMBALAYA

1 cup uncooked regular rice
¼ cup bacon drippings
1 small onion, chopped
1 medium-size green pepper, chopped
1 bunch green onions, chopped
3 tablespoons chopped fresh parsley
1 cup chopped cooked ham
1 tablespoon vegetable oil
2 cups chicken broth
1 (14½-ounce) can whole tomatoes, undrained
1 bay leaf
1 clove garlic, minced
½ teaspoon ground thyme
⅛ teaspoon pepper
5 dashes hot sauce
2 cups chopped cooked chicken

Cook rice in drippings in a small cast-iron skillet, stirring frequently, until rice is lightly browned. Set aside.

Sauté onion, green pepper, green onions, parsley, and ham in oil in a Dutch oven until vegetables are tender. Stir in browned rice. Add broth, tomatoes, bay leaf, garlic, thyme, pepper, and hot sauce; stir until blended. Cover and cook over low heat 1 hour or until liquid is absorbed. Stir in chicken. Yield: 6 to 8 servings.

CHICKEN WIGGLE

2 (2½- to 3-pound) broiler-fryers, cut up
2 medium onions, chopped
½ cup chopped celery
2 fresh celery leaves, chopped
¼ cup finely chopped fresh parsley
1 tablespoon salt
1 medium-size green pepper, chopped
1 cup uncooked regular rice
1 (28-ounce) can whole tomatoes, drained and chopped
1 (8-ounce) can sliced mushrooms, drained
1 (3-ounce) jar pimiento-stuffed olives, sliced
1 (17-ounce) can English peas, drained (optional)

Combine first 6 ingredients in a large Dutch oven. Add enough water to cover chicken; bring to a boil. Reduce heat, and simmer 1 hour or until chicken is tender. Remove chicken from broth, and cool; strain broth, reserving 1 cup. Remove chicken from bones, and coarsely chop meat. Set aside.

Combine reserved broth, green pepper, rice, and tomatoes in a medium saucepan; bring to a boil. Cover; reduce heat, and simmer 25 minutes or until liquid is absorbed.

Combine chicken, rice mixture, mushrooms, olives, and peas, if desired. Stir well, and spoon mixture into a lightly greased 13- x 9- x 2-inch baking dish. Bake, uncovered, at 350° for 30 to 40 minutes. Yield: 8 to 10 servings.

TURN-OF-THE-CENTURY CHICKEN PILAU

4 cups chopped cooked chicken
7 cups chicken broth, divided
4 cups uncooked regular rice
4 hard-cooked eggs, chopped
7 slices bacon, cooked and crumbled
1 teaspoon salt
½ teaspoon pepper

Combine chicken and 2 cups broth; cover and set aside.

Combine remaining broth, rice, eggs, bacon, and seasonings in a Dutch oven; bring to a boil. Reduce heat; cover and simmer 35 minutes or until liquid is absorbed.

Drain chicken, and gently stir into cooked rice mixture. Cover and let stand 15 minutes or until chicken is thoroughly heated. Spoon into serving dish. Yield: 8 to 10 servings.

CHARLESTON CHICKEN PILAF

½ cup butter or margarine
1 (2½- to 3-pound) broiler-fryer, cut up
1 medium onion, chopped
1 cup diced celery
2 cups uncooked regular rice
1 quart chicken broth
½ teaspoon salt
¼ teaspoon pepper
⅛ teaspoon ground nutmeg

Melt butter in a heavy oven-proof Dutch oven; add chicken, and brown on all sides. Add onion and celery; simmer until vegetables are tender, stirring frequently. Stir in remaining ingredients; bring to a boil.

Bake, covered, at 350° for 20 minutes. Yield: 6 servings.

MOTHER'S CHICKEN SPAGHETTI

1 (3½- to 4-pound) broiler-fryer, cut up
1½ teaspoons salt, divided
1 (28-ounce) can whole tomatoes, undrained
¼ cup plus 3 tablespoons butter or margarine, divided
3 tablespoons all-purpose flour
½ cup whipping cream
⅛ teaspoon ground nutmeg
⅛ teaspoon pepper
¼ pound ground beef
¼ pound bulk pork sausage
½ pound fresh mushrooms, sliced
2 cups finely chopped onion
1½ cups finely chopped celery
1½ cups chopped green pepper
2 cloves garlic, minced
1 bay leaf
½ teaspoon dried red pepper flakes
1 (16-ounce) package spaghetti
2 cups (8 ounces) sharp Cheddar cheese
Grated Parmesan cheese

Place chicken, 1 teaspoon salt, and water to cover in a Dutch oven. Bring to a boil; cover and simmer 45 minutes. Remove chicken from broth; cool, reserving 2½ cups broth. Bone chicken, and cut meat into bite-size pieces. Set aside.

Place tomatoes in a heavy saucepan. Bring to a boil; reduce heat, and simmer 15 minutes. Set aside.

Melt 3 tablespoons butter in a heavy saucepan over low heat; add flour, stirring until smooth. Cook 1 minute, stirring constantly. Gradually stir in cream and 1 cup reserved broth; cook over medium heat, stirring constantly, until thickened and bubbly. Stir in nutmeg, pepper, and remaining salt. Set aside.

Combine beef and sausage in a medium skillet; cook over medium heat until meat is browned, stirring to crumble. Drain and set aside.

Sauté mushrooms, onion, celery, green pepper, and garlic in remaining butter in a Dutch oven 5 minutes or until vegetables are crisp-tender. Add tomatoes, white sauce, meat, bay leaf, and red pepper flakes to Dutch oven; stir well. Simmer over low heat 15 minutes. Discard bay leaf. Cook spaghetti according to package directions; drain and set aside.

Spoon one-third of meat sauce into a lightly greased 5-quart casserole. Top with half of spaghetti, half of chicken, one-third of meat sauce, and half of Cheddar cheese. Repeat layers, beginning with spaghetti and ending with Cheddar cheese. Pour remaining reserved broth over layers. Bake, covered, at 350° for 15 minutes. Uncover and bake an additional 15 minutes. Serve with Parmesan cheese. Yield: 12 servings.

ALABAMA CHICKEN SPAGHETTI

2 (14½-ounce) cans whole tomatoes, undrained and chopped
1 (12-ounce) can tomato paste
1 (6-ounce) can sliced mushrooms, undrained
4 cups cubed cooked chicken
2 cups water
1¼ cups chopped celery
¼ cup Worcestershire sauce
5 small onions, chopped
4 cloves garlic, minced
3 medium-size green peppers, chopped
3 bay leaves
2 teaspoons paprika
½ teaspoon rubbed sage
¼ teaspoon pepper
⅛ teaspoon red pepper
⅛ teaspoon ground ginger
Hot cooked spaghetti

Combine all ingredients except spaghetti in a large Dutch oven; cover and simmer 2 hours. Uncover and simmer 2 additional hours, stirring occasionally. Discard bay leaves. Serve sauce over spaghetti. Yield: 8 to 10 servings.

The South is justly famous for its "chicken and" dishes. Quite aside from our kettle-cooked one dish meals served in bowls, we have a history of chicken combinations that stretch to make filling main dishes for family entertaining. If they are rooted in austerity or learned during hard times, it matters not—these dishes today are fit to grace the most elegant table. Chicken and pasta comprise one time-honored way to make poultry go a long way. Remember Thomas Jefferson's admiration of European foods? The pasta of Naples so intrigued him on a visit there that he had crates of it shipped home in the late 1700s. Luisa Tetrazzini's coloratura voice so enchanted Americans on her early 1900s tour that some unnamed chef created a chicken dish in her honor. Her repertoire covered forty operas; there may be that many versions of Tetrazzini.

Collection of Business Americana

Mother's Chicken Spaghetti

PANHANDLE CHICKEN SPAGHETTI

1 (3- to 3½-pound)
  broiler-fryer, cut up
1 (8-ounce) package thin
  spaghetti
2 small onions, chopped
½ cup chopped celery
1 small clove garlic, minced
1½ tablespoons vegetable oil
1 tablespoon flour
1 (16-ounce) can whole
  tomatoes, drained and
  chopped
¼ teaspoon Worcestershire
  sauce
2 to 2½ teaspoons chili
  powder
1½ teaspoons sugar
⅛ teaspoon salt
⅛ teaspoon pepper
½ pound medium shrimp,
  peeled and deveined
1 (4½-ounce) jar sliced
  mushrooms, drained
1 cup grated Parmesan
  cheese, divided
1 tablespoon butter or
  margarine

Place chicken in a Dutch oven; add water to cover. Bring to a boil; cover and simmer 1 hour or until tender. Remove chicken from broth; cool. Reserve 1 cup broth. Bone chicken, and coarsely chop.

Cook spaghetti according to package directions; drain and set aside.

Sauté onion, celery, and garlic in oil in a large Dutch oven until tender. Add flour; cook until bubbly. Stir in tomatoes and reserved broth; bring to a boil. Add Worcestershire sauce, seasonings, shrimp, mushrooms, and reserved chicken; mix well. Gently fold spaghetti into chicken mixture.

Spoon half of spaghetti-chicken mixture into a greased, shallow 2½-quart casserole. Sprinkle with ½ cup Parmesan cheese. Top with remaining spaghetti mixture. Dot with butter; cover and bake at 350° for 30 minutes. Sprinkle with remaining Parmesan cheese; bake, uncovered, 15 minutes. Yield: 6 to 8 servings.

PARTY CHICKEN SPAGHETTI

1 (4½- to 5-pound) baking
  hen
3 quarts water
2 teaspoons salt, divided
1 (12-ounce) package thin
  spaghetti
2 medium onions, chopped
2 medium-size green peppers,
  chopped
½ teaspoon curry
  powder
¼ teaspoon pepper
1 (14½-ounce) can whole
  tomatoes, undrained
1 (8-ounce) can mushroom
  pieces and stems, drained
1 (4-ounce) jar chopped
  pimiento, drained
2 cups (8 ounces) shredded
  extra-sharp Cheddar
  cheese
¼ cup grated Parmesan
  cheese

Place chicken in a large Dutch oven; add water to cover. Bring to a boil; cover and simmer 1½ hours or until chicken is tender. Remove chicken from Dutch oven, reserving 2 cups broth. Bone chicken; chop meat, and set aside.

Bring water and 1 teaspoon salt to a boil in a heavy saucepan. Gradually stir in spaghetti; return water to boil. Boil 9 to 11 minutes; drain and set aside.

Add onion, green pepper, curry powder, remaining salt, and pepper to reserved broth in Dutch oven. Bring to a boil; cover and simmer 10 minutes or until vegetables are tender. Add tomatoes, mushrooms, and pimientos; cook, uncovered, until thoroughly heated.

Spoon half of cooked spaghetti into a buttered 2½-quart casserole; top with half each of chopped chicken, tomato mixture, and shredded Cheddar cheese. Repeat layers with remaining spaghetti, chopped chicken, and tomato mixture. Bake at 350° for 50 minutes. Add remaining Cheddar and Parmesan cheese, and bake an additional 10 minutes or until cheese melts. Yield: 10 servings.

Cooks in the making at Virginia Girls Canning and Poultry Club, 1913.

Weathercock, used atop barns to indicate wind direction.

CHICKEN TETRAZZINI

1 (2½- to 3-pound) broiler-fryer
2 celery stalks, cut into large pieces
1 medium onion, sliced
1½ teaspoons salt
1 quart water
3 tablespoons all-purpose flour
2 egg yolks, beaten
½ cup whipping cream
½ pound fresh mushrooms, sliced
½ teaspoon salt
1 (12-ounce) package thin spaghetti
3 tablespoons grated Parmesan cheese
1 tablespoon butter or margarine

Combine chicken, celery, onion, salt, and water in a Dutch oven. Bring to a boil; cover and simmer 1 hour or until chicken is tender. Remove chicken from broth; cool. Remove chicken from bones; chop meat, and set aside. Strain broth; discard vegetables. Refrigerate broth until all fat has risen to the top; skim off fat, and set aside. Reserve remaining broth.

Melt 3 tablespoons reserved fat in a heavy saucepan over low heat; add flour, stirring until smooth. Cook 1 minute, stirring constantly. Gradually add 1½ cups of reserved broth; set remaining broth aside. Cook over medium heat, stirring constantly, until thickened and bubbly. Combine egg yolks and cream; stir well. Gradually stir about one-fourth of hot mixture into egg mixture; stir into remaining hot mixture. Cook over medium heat, stirring constantly, until mixture is smooth and thickened.

Sauté mushrooms in remaining fat 2 minutes. Add sautéed mushrooms, salt, and chicken to cream sauce; stir well.

Cook spaghetti according to package directions in remaining broth plus enough water to equal 3 quarts liquid.

Drain spaghetti, and place in a 10-inch pieplate. Spoon chicken mixture over top; sprinkle with Parmesan cheese, and dot with butter. Broil 6 inches from heat 5 minutes or just until cheese is lightly browned. Yield: 6 servings.

73

BEFORE THE COLONEL

Southern Favorites: Fried and Barbecued

Yes, there was fried chicken before the universal red-striped cardboard carton, symbol of the late Colonel Harland Sanders. His story may have been from too ragged to too rich even for Horatio Alger had he been alive to write the story: Poor Kentucky boy scrapes money to open his tiny roadside eatery at Corbin in eastern Kentucky. Decades pass; money pours in. Sanders, in white beard, white suit, and black string tie becomes the most easily recognized figure in any international airport. Sanders is remembered not only for the fortune he made from chicken, but for his honest kind of down-home charm, his philanthropies, and his salty stories.

But that ubiquitous striped pail wasn't in the rumble seat of the Model A car when Grandad took his best girl for a picnic in the park. It was home-fried chicken they carried in their hamper. And no commercially fried chicken at the box supper he attended fifty or more years ago—only that beautifully wrapped supper his chosen lady had prepared for him.

Along with fried chicken, our grandmother-to-be had filled her box with her specialties: biscuits, homemade pickles, potato salad with cooked dressing, and always his favorite pie or cake. Lucky the girl who could find a round or oval hat box; crepe paper and ribbon added, it was such a work of art that an imperfect morsel could go unnoticed.

Oven-fried chicken is a twentieth-century development. Boon to weight watchers and the cholesterol conscious, oven-fried chicken can be prepared in such a way as to be very nearly fat-free. Start by discarding the skin even if the recipe does not call for this procedure. Egg white, slightly beaten, can be used instead of a whole egg for dipping the pieces between the flour and crumb coatings. Mixed herbs can be substituted for the salt for salt-free dieters. And oven-fried chicken doesn't have to be watched, just committed to the oven while a timer ticks off the cooking time.

Oven-barbecued chicken is a satisfying dish...in winter. However, it lacks that one ingredient we can have only out-of-doors: smoke. What better dish than chicken barbecued on the open grill!

Fair weather was made for picnics, so drive, hike, or bike to some special place in the park or on a lake. Checklist: Southern Fried Chicken, Mustard Potato Salad, Deviled Eggs, Pickled Green Beans, and Lemonade "made in the shade and stirred with a spade."

PICNIC IN THE PARK

The picnic, in various guises, has held its place through the centuries. In the early 1800s, a fashionable group in London formed The Picnic Society for the purpose of taking excursions and holding private theatricals, each member bringing his share of the refreshments. The original purpose of the Society's picnic was meeting and sharing food, not necessarily outdoors.

When we think now of a picnic, we assume the outdoors as an ingredient, and everyone brings. Inevitably fried chicken turns up in those hampers. It is one of the few portable meats that's as good cold as hot. And each piece comes with a handle on it . . . ever so practical.

SOUTHERN FRIED CHICKEN
MUSTARD POTATO SALAD
DEVILED EGGS
MARINATED COLE SLAW
PICKLED GREEN BEANS
HOMEMADE VANILLA ICE CREAM
PEACH COBBLER
LEMONDADE

Serves 8

SOUTHERN FRIED CHICKEN

2 (3- to 3½-pound)
   broiler-fryers, cut up
2 teaspoons salt, divided
1⅔ cups all-purpose flour
1½ teaspoons baking powder
Vegetable oil

Rub chicken pieces with 1 teaspoon salt; set aside.

Combine flour, baking powder, and remaining 1 teaspoon salt in a plastic or paper bag; shake to mix well. Place 2 or 3 pieces of chicken in bag; shake well. Repeat procedure with remaining chicken.

Heat 3 to 4 inches of oil to 375°; add chicken, and fry until golden brown. Drain on paper towels. Yield: 8 servings.

MUSTARD POTATO SALAD

5 medium potatoes
½ cup mayonnaise
2 tablespoons prepared
   mustard
3 hard-cooked eggs, coarsely
   chopped
1 cup diagonally sliced celery
   (¼-inch slices)
1 small onion, chopped
¼ cup sweet pickle relish
2 tablespoons chopped green
   pepper
½ teaspoon salt
¼ teaspoon pepper
Green pepper rings
Pimiento strips

Cook potatoes in boiling salted water 20 minutes or until tender. Drain well, and cool slightly. Peel and cut potatoes into ¾-inch cubes.

Combine mayonnaise and mustard; stir well. Add potatoes; toss to coat well. Gently fold in next 7 ingredients; chill at least 2 hours. Garnish with green pepper and pimiento. Yield: 8 servings.

A dashing new touring car, just the thing to take a picnic to the countryside.

1900 ad for poultry feed

DEVILED EGGS

12 hard-cooked eggs
⅓ cup mayonnaise
1 tablespoon prepared
   mustard
¼ teaspoon salt
⅛ teaspoon red pepper
12 pimiento-stuffed olives,
   sliced
Fresh parsley sprigs

Slice eggs in half lengthwise, and carefully remove yolks. Mash yolks with mayonnaise. Add mustard, salt, and pepper; stir well. Stuff egg whites with yolk mixture. Garnish eggs with olive slices and parsley. Yield: 8 to 10 servings.

Someone had to invent the picnic, so it should come as no surprise to find that the Greeks did it. It was the custom for men of letters to hold reunions, probably to discuss philosophy, with each member of the club providing a part of the meal. Rome, as always quick to absorb lessons from the Greeks, followed suit. The poet Horace left accounts of picnics and the pleasure he took in them.

MARINATED COLE SLAW

1 medium cabbage, finely
   shredded
1 medium onion, chopped
1 medium-size green pepper,
   chopped
1 (4-ounce) jar diced
   pimiento, drained
½ cup vinegar
½ cup vegetable oil
½ cup honey
2 teaspoons sugar
2 teaspoons salt

Combine first 4 ingredients in a large bowl; set aside.

Combine remaining ingredients in a medium saucepan; bring to a boil. Pour over vegetables, stirring well. Cover and refrigerate up to 3 days before serving. Yield: 8 to 10 servings.

PICKLED GREEN BEANS

1 cup sugar
1 cup vinegar
½ cup vegetable oil
2 tablespoons sweet pickle
   juice
1 tablespoon water
1 teaspoon salt
¼ teaspoon pepper
2 (16-ounce) cans cut green
   beans, drained
1 medium-size purple onion,
   thinly sliced
1 medium-size green pepper,
   cut into thin lengthwise
   strips
4 stalks celery, cut into thin
   lengthwise strips
4 green onions, finely
   chopped
1 (4-ounce) jar diced
   pimiento, drained

Combine first 7 ingredients in a medium saucepan; bring to a boil, stirring well. Remove from heat, and cool.

Combine remaining ingredients in a large bowl. Pour vinegar mixture over vegetables; toss gently to coat well. Cover and refrigerate overnight. Drain vegetables before serving. Yield: 8 servings.

PEACH COBBLER

Pie Strip Pastry
5 cups sliced fresh peaches
  (about 10 medium peaches)
1½ cups water
½ cup butter or margarine
1½ cups sugar
2 tablespoons all-purpose
  flour
¼ teaspoon ground
  cinnamon
Pinch of salt
1 tablespoon sugar

Roll out Pie Strip Pastry to ⅛-inch thickness on a lightly floured surface; cut into 1-inch strips. Reserve enough strips to lattice top of cobbler. Place remaining strips on baking sheet, and bake at 450° for 10 minutes or until crisp. Remove strips from baking sheet; set aside.

Combine peaches, water, and butter in a medium saucepan; bring to a boil, and cook over low heat until peaches are tender. Combine 1½ cups sugar, flour, cinnamon, and salt; add to peach mixture. Cook over low heat, stirring gently until sugar dissolves and mixture thickens.

Pour half the peach mixture into a lightly greased 12- x 8- x 2-inch baking dish. Arrange baked pastry strips on top of peach mixture. Spoon remaining peach mixture over pastry strips in baking dish. Arrange unbaked pastry strips in lattice design over peaches. Sprinkle with 1 tablespoon sugar. Bake at 375° for 35 to 40 minutes. Yield: 8 servings.

Has someone gone for ice and salt? Children are waiting.

HOMEMADE VANILLA ICE CREAM

6 eggs
1½ cups sugar
⅛ teaspoon salt
7 cups half-and-half, divided
1 tablespoon vanilla extract

Beat eggs in a heavy saucepan; add sugar, salt, and 2 cups half-and-half. Cook over medium heat, stirring constantly until smooth and thickened. (Mixture should coat a metal spoon.) Remove custard from heat, and stir in vanilla. Cool completely.

Combine custard and remaining half-and-half; mix well. Pour into freezer can of a 1-gallon hand-turned or electric freezer; freeze according to manufacturer's instructions. Let ripen at least 1 hour. Yield: 1 gallon.

Pie Strip Pastry:

2 cups all-purpose flour
½ teaspoon salt
1 cup shortening
¼ cup plus 2 tablespoons
  cold water

Combine flour and salt; cut in shortening until mixture resembles coarse meal. Sprinkle water over flour mixture, and stir with a fork until ingredients are moistened. Shape pastry into a ball; chill. Yield: pastry for 1 cobbler.

CRISP AND CRUNCHY

DEEP-FAT FRIED CHICKEN

½ cup all-purpose flour
2 teaspoons salt
½ teaspoon pepper
1 (3- to 3½-pound)
  broiler-fryer, cut up
Vegetable oil

Combine flour, salt, and pepper; dredge chicken pieces in flour mixture. Deep fry in hot oil (375°) 15 minutes or until golden brown. Drain chicken well on paper towels. Yield: 4 servings.

As farm women have done down through the years, Mrs. McClelland positions frying chicken in an iron skillet. Escambia Farms, Florida, June, 1942.

GOLDEN CHICKEN NUGGETS

3 whole chicken breasts,
  skinned and boned
½ cup all-purpose flour
½ cup water
1 egg, slightly beaten
2 teaspoons sesame
  seeds
¾ teaspoon salt
Vegetable oil
½ cup honey
⅓ cup Dijon mustard

Cut chicken into 1- x 1½-inch pieces; set aside. Combine next 5 ingredients; mix well. Dip chicken into batter, and fry in hot oil (375°) until golden brown. Drain on paper towels. Combine honey and mustard, stirring well. Serve with nuggets. Yield: 4 servings.

I t is doubtful if any dish is as over-exposed and as poorly presented as the so-called Southern Fried Chicken. It can be one of the tastiest methods of preparing chicken, or it can be a complete flop. Real southern fried chicken is not necessarily loaded with a heavy crust. It may be lightly seasoned with salt and pepper, coated with flour, and fried in the skillet. The end product should be very tender, moist, and cooked through and through.

CRUMB-COATED FRIED CHICKEN

1 cup finely crushed cracker
  crumbs
1 teaspoon salt
1 teaspoon pepper
1 egg, beaten
1 (3- to 3½-pound)
  broiler-fryer, cut up
Vegetable oil

Combine first 3 ingredients; mix well. Dip chicken in egg; dredge in crumb mixture.
Heat 1 inch of oil in a large skillet to 325°; add chicken, and fry 30 minutes or until golden brown, turning once. Drain chicken on paper towels. Yield: 4 servings.

GARLIC FRIED CHICKEN

1 (8-ounce) carton
  commercial sour cream
2 tablespoons lemon juice
1 clove garlic, crushed
½ teaspoon paprika
¼ teaspoon celery salt
½ teaspoon salt
¼ teaspoon pepper
¼ teaspoon Worcestershire
  sauce
2 (2½- to 3-pound)
  broiler-fryers, cut up
1⅔ cups all-purpose flour
Vegetable oil

Combine first 8 ingredients; mix well. Place chicken in a shallow pan, and pour sour cream mixture over top. Cover and refrigerate overnight.

Remove chicken from liquid. Dredge chicken in flour.

Heat 1 inch of oil in a large skillet to 325°; add chicken and fry 15 to 20 minutes, turning once. Drain chicken well on paper towels. Yield: 8 servings.

Garlic Fried Chicken: An interesting and flavorful variation.

BUTTERY FRIED CHICKEN

1 (3- to 3½-pound)
  broiler-fryer, cut up
1½ teaspoons salt
1 cup all-purpose flour
1 cup bacon drippings
¼ cup butter, divided

Soak chicken in cold salted water at least 30 minutes. Drain and pat dry; sprinkle with salt. Place flour in a plastic or paper bag; add 2 or 3 pieces of chicken, and shake well. Repeat procedure with remaining chicken.

Heat bacon drippings in a large skillet to 375°; add chicken and 1 teaspoon butter. Fry 30 minutes, turning once; add a small amount of remaining butter at regular intervals throughout frying process. Drain chicken on paper towels. Yield: 4 servings.

CRUSTY BUTTERMILK FRIED CHICKEN

1 (3- to 3½-pound)
  broiler-fryer, cut up
2 cups buttermilk
1 cup self-rising flour
1½ teaspoons salt
1 teaspoon pepper
Vegetable oil

Place chicken in a shallow pan, and pour buttermilk over top; cover and refrigerate overnight or at least 8 hours.

Remove chicken from liquid. Combine flour, salt, and pepper in a plastic or paper bag; shake to mix. Place 2 or 3 pieces of chicken in bag, and shake well. Repeat procedure with remaining chicken.

Heat 1 inch of oil in a large skillet to 325°; add chicken and fry 20 minutes or until golden brown, turning once. Drain on paper towels. Yield: 4 servings.

CRISPY FRIED SQUAB

6 squabs, split
2 teaspoons salt
1 teaspoon pepper
1 cup all-purpose flour
4 cups shortening

Sprinkle squabs with salt and pepper; dredge in flour.

Heat shortening to 325°; add squabs, and fry 15 minutes or until golden brown and crisp, turning frequently. Drain well on paper towels before serving. Yield: 4 to 6 servings.

COVERED AND FRIED

BATTER FRIED CHICKEN

1 cup all-purpose flour
1 teaspoon baking powder
1 teaspoon salt
¼ teaspoon pepper
1 egg, beaten
¾ cup milk
1 (3½- to 4-pound)
  broiler-fryer, cut up
Vegetable oil

Combine first 6 ingredients; mix well. Dip chicken pieces into batter.

Heat 1 inch of oil in a large skillet to 375°; add chicken, and brown quickly on all sides. Reduce heat; cover, and fry 25 minutes or until chicken is tender and golden brown, turning occasionally. Drain well on paper towels. Yield: 4 servings.

J.D. Calhoun's Jersey Red Chicken Farm, Sumpter, Louisiana, 1905.

COUNTRY-FRIED CHICKEN

½ cup all-purpose flour
½ teaspoon paprika
1 teaspoon salt
¼ teaspoon pepper
1 (3- to 3½-pound)
  broiler-fryer, cut up
Vegetable oil

Combine first 4 ingredients in a plastic or paper bag; shake to mix. Place 2 or 3 pieces of chicken in bag; shake well. Repeat procedure with remaining chicken.

Heat ½ inch of oil in a large skillet to 350°; add chicken, and brown on all sides. Reduce heat to medium; cover, and cook 30 minutes or until chicken is tender.

Remove cover, and cook an additional 10 minutes, turning occasionally. Drain well on paper towels. Yield: 4 servings.

SAVANNAH FRIED CHICKEN

⅔ cup buttermilk
1 teaspoon salt
½ teaspoon hot sauce
1 (3- to 3½-pound)
  broiler-fryer, cut up
1 cup all-purpose flour
Vegetable oil

Combine first 3 ingredients; mix well. Place chicken in a shallow pan, and pour buttermilk mixture over top; refrigerate at least 15 minutes.

Remove chicken from liquid. Dredge chicken in flour.

Heat ½ inch of oil in a skillet to 350°; add chicken and cook, turning frequently, until chicken is brown on all sides. Reduce heat to medium; cover, and cook 25 minutes or until chicken is tender, turning occasionally. Drain well on paper towels. Yield: 4 servings.

BUTTERMILK FRIED CHICKEN

2 cups buttermilk
1½ teaspoons salt
½ teaspoon pepper
1 (3- to 3½-pound) broiler-fryer, cut up and skinned
1 cup self-rising flour
½ teaspoon ground thyme
Vegetable oil

Combine first 3 ingredients. Pour buttermilk mixture over top of chicken. Cover, and refrigerate at least 30 minutes. Remove chicken from liquid.

Combine flour and thyme, stirring well. Dredge chicken in flour mixture.

Heat 1 inch of oil in a large skillet to 350°. Add chicken; cover, and fry 25 minutes or until golden brown, turning once. Drain chicken on paper towels. Yield: 4 servings.

TEXAS-STYLE FRIED CHICKEN

1 teaspoon salt
¼ teaspoon pepper
1 (2½- to 3-pound) broiler-fryer, cut up
½ cup all-purpose flour
4 cups shortening

Sprinkle salt and pepper over chicken; dredge in flour.

Heat shortening in a large skillet to 350°; add chicken, and fry 5 minutes or until golden brown, turning once. Reduce heat; cover and continue cooking 15 minutes or until tender, turning as necessary. Uncover, and cook an additional 5 minutes. Drain on paper towels. Yield: 4 servings.

FRIED ROCK CORNISH HENS

½ cup all-purpose flour
2 teaspoons paprika
2 teaspoons salt
½ teaspoon pepper
2 (1- to 1½-pound) Cornish hens, split
⅔ cup butter or margarine
2 tablespoons water

Combine first 4 ingredients in a plastic or paper bag; shake to mix. Add Cornish hens, and shake well.

Melt butter in a large skillet over medium heat. Add Cornish hens; brown slowly for 15 minutes, turning as necessary. Reduce heat. Add water; cover and cook 15 minutes or until Cornish hens are golden brown. Uncover, and cook an additional 5 minutes. Drain on paper towels. Yield: 2 to 4 servings.

Fried Rock Cornish Hens, buttery flavored and guest-worthy.

CREOLE FRIED DUCKLING

1 cup all-purpose flour
2 teaspoons paprika
2 teaspoons salt
¼ teaspoon pepper
1 (4- to 4½-pound) dressed
  duckling, cut up
¼ cup butter or margarine
Melted shortening
¼ cup water

Combine flour, salt, paprika, and pepper; mix well. Dredge duckling in flour mixture.

Melt butter in a large skillet over low heat; add melted shortening to equal a ¼-inch depth in skillet. Heat butter and shortening to 350°; add duckling, and fry until golden brown, turning frequently.

Reduce heat to low; add water. Cover and cook for 30 minutes or until duckling is tender. Yield: 4 servings.

Maryland Fried Chicken: meltingly tender.

Т he disservice done the public by commercially fried chicken is perpetuating the fallacy that Southern fried, by definition, is crisp, crunchy, and deep fried. There is more to it than that, for there are other ways to fry a chicken.

So how does a Southerner fry chicken at home? He coats the disjointed chicken with seasoned flour and browns it in hot shortening or oil on both sides. Now for the decision: to crisp or not to crisp? With lid on and heat lowered, the chicken becomes meltingly tender, not the least bit crisp, and as Southern as any other. This can be carried a step further: when the chicken is done, excess fat may be poured off, and a little water added. Lid on again for five minutes of steam, and there's Southern fried fit for the gods.

MARYLAND FRIED CHICKEN WITH CREAM GRAVY

1 cup all-purpose
  flour
1 teaspoon salt
¼ teaspoon paprika
1 (2- to 2½-pound)
  broiler-fryer, cut up
Vegetable oil
¼ cup water
1 tablespoon butter or
  margarine
1 cup milk

Combine first 3 ingredients in a plastic or paper bag; shake to mix. Place 2 or 3 pieces of chicken in bag; shake well. Repeat procedure with remaining chicken. Reserve 2 tablespoons seasoned flour for gravy.

Heat ½ inch of oil in a large skillet to 325°; add chicken. Cover, and cook 7 minutes.

Turn chicken; cover, and cook an additional 7 minutes. Reduce heat; drain off oil, reserving 2 tablespoons oil and chicken in skillet. Add water to skillet; cover and continue cooking over low heat 20 minutes or until tender. Drain chicken on paper towels; transfer to a warmed serving platter.

Add butter to pan drippings, and melt. Scrape sides of skillet with a wooden spoon to loosen browned crumbs. Gradually add reserved flour mixture, stirring until smooth. Cook 1 minute, stirring constantly. Gradually add milk; cook over medium heat, stirring constantly, until thickened and bubbly. Serve gravy with chicken. Yield: 4 servings.

Recipes for fried chicken are not startlingly different from one section of the South to another; the differences are more from cook to cook than from state to state—and specifically, from those cooks who "never make gravy" to those who do. To many Southerners, nothing is better than chicken, fried to perfection, steamed for tenderness, and served up with a rich cream gravy made from the crusty morsels remaining in the skillet after the chicken has been fried. Simply pour off the excess fat and add a little flour to the skillet. Brown the flour, scraping up the crust from the bottom of the skillet as you go. Stir in some milk and cook until the gravy "pops."

Some Southerners like to make "chicken biscuits." Once the chicken is fried and before the fat is poured away to make ready for the gravy, make a batch of baking powder biscuits and fry them in the hot grease. If the grease does not cover them, turn them over once. Drown the biscuits in the gravy and serve with your fried chicken.

OLD DOMINION FRIED CHICKEN WITH GRAVY

¾ cup all-purpose flour
1 teaspoon salt
¼ teaspoon pepper
1 (2½- to 3-pound)
  broiler-fryer, cut up
1 cup shortening
1 cup milk

Combine first 3 ingredients in a plastic or paper bag; shake to mix. Place 2 or 3 pieces of chicken in bag; shake well. Repeat procedure with remaining chicken. Set 2 tablespoons seasoned flour aside.

Heat shortening in a large skillet to 350°; add chicken, and fry 5 minutes, turning frequently to brown on all sides. Reduce heat; cover and cook an additional 25 minutes or until tender and golden brown, turning once. Drain on paper towels.

Drain off pan drippings, reserving 2 tablespoons in skillet. Add reserved flour, stirring until smooth. Cook 1 minute, stirring constantly. Gradually add milk; cook over medium heat, stirring constantly, until thickened and bubbly. Serve gravy with fried chicken. Yield: 4 servings.

FRIED CHICKEN WITH SAW MILL GRAVY

½ cup all-purpose
  flour
1 teaspoon salt
¼ teaspoon pepper
1 (2½- to 3-pound)
  broiler-fryer, cut up
1 cup lard
1½ cups milk
1 tablespoon chopped
  fresh parsley

Combine first 3 ingredients in a plastic or paper bag; shake to mix. Place 2 or 3 pieces of chicken in bag; shake well. Repeat procedure with remaining chicken.

Heat lard in a large skillet to 325°; add chicken, and fry 8 minutes or until golden brown, turning once. Reduce heat; cover and continue cooking 15 minutes or until chicken is tender. Remove chicken; drain on paper towels.

Drain off pan drippings, reserving 2 tablespoons in skillet. Return chicken to skillet, and pour milk over top. Sprinkle with parsley. Cook, uncovered, over low heat 15 minutes or until gravy is thickened and bubbly. Serve gravy with chicken. Yield: 4 servings.

COASTAL FRIED CHICKEN WITH BROWN CRUMB GRAVY

1 (3- to 3½-pound)
  broiler-fryer, cut up
1 teaspoon salt
¼ teaspoon pepper
1 cup all-purpose flour
Vegetable oil
Hot cooked rice
Brown Crumb Gravy

Sprinkle chicken with salt and pepper; dredge in flour.

Heat 2 inches of oil in a large skillet to 350°; add chicken. Cover and fry 30 minutes or until golden brown, turning once. Reserve 2 tablespoons drippings in skillet for gravy. Drain chicken on paper towels. Serve with rice and Brown Crumb Gravy. Yield: 4 servings.

Brown Crumb Gravy:

2 tablespoons all-purpose
  flour
2 tablespoons reserved pan
  drippings
2 cups water
¼ teaspoon salt
⅛ teaspoon pepper

Add flour to pan drippings in skillet; cook over medium heat, scraping sides of skillet with a wooden spoon to loosen browned crumbs. Gradually add water, stirring constantly, until thickened and bubbly. Stir in salt and pepper. Yield: 1½ cups.

Coastal Fried Chicken: If it is served with rice, you know for sure you're down South. Well-cooked Brown Crumb Gravy is the proper crowning touch.

FROM OVEN AND GRILL

OVEN-FRIED CHICKEN

1 cup finely crushed cracker
  crumbs
2 teaspoons paprika
2 teaspoons salt
¼ teaspoon pepper
1 (2½- to 3-pound)
  broiler-fryer, cut up
¼ cup butter or margarine,
  melted

Combine cracker crumbs, paprika, salt, and pepper; mix well. Dip chicken in butter; dredge in crumb mixture, and place in a lightly greased 13- x 9- x 2-inch baking dish. Bake, uncovered, at 350° for 1 hour and 10 minutes. Yield: 4 servings.

Note: To achieve a golden color, dredge chicken in finely crushed corn flakes.

PECAN OVEN-FRIED CHICKEN

1 cup finely chopped
  pecans
½ cup all-purpose flour
1 (3- to 3½-pound)
  broiler-fryer, cut up and
  skinned
1 teaspoon salt
1 teaspoon paprika
½ cup evaporated milk
¼ cup butter or margarine,
  melted

Combine first 4 ingredients; stir well. Dip chicken in milk, and dredge in pecan mixture. Place chicken in a 13- x 9- x 2-inch baking dish; pour butter over top. Bake at 375° for 1 hour or until chicken is tender. Yield: 4 servings.

TEXAS OVEN-FRIED CHICKEN

1 cup all-purpose flour
1½ teaspoons salt
1 teaspoon pepper
1 (2½- to 3-pound)
  broiler-fryer, cut up
1 cup boiling water

Combine first 3 ingredients; mix well. Dredge chicken in flour mixture, and place in a lightly greased 13- x 9- x 2-inch baking pan. Pour boiling water over chicken. Bake at 375° for 15 minutes.

Broil 6 inches from heat for 10 minutes or just until chicken is lightly browned.

Reduce heat to 275°, and continue baking for 1 hour and 30 minutes. Yield: 4 servings.

HERBED OVEN-FRIED CHICKEN

½ cup all-purpose flour
½ cup fine, dry breadcrumbs
1 teaspoon paprika
1 teaspoon salt
¼ teaspoon pepper
¼ teaspoon ground thyme
1 (3- to 3½-pound)
  broiler-fryer, cut up
¼ cup butter or margarine,
  melted
1 tablespoon vegetable oil

Combine first 6 ingredients in a plastic or paper bag; shake to mix. Place 2 or 3 chicken pieces in bag; shake well, and set aside. Repeat procedure with remaining chicken.

Pour butter and oil in a 12- x 8- x 2-inch baking dish; add chicken pieces. Bake, uncovered, at 400° for 30 minutes. Turn chicken; reduce heat to 350°, and bake an additional 15 minutes or until chicken is tender. Yield: 4 servings.

Pecan Oven-Fried Chicken: Just bake and serve it up.

PAPER SACK CHICKEN BARBECUE

3 tablespoons brown sugar
1 teaspoon dry mustard
1 teaspoon paprika
1 teaspoon chili powder
1 teaspoon salt
½ teaspoon pepper
¼ cup water
3 tablespoons catsup
2 tablespoons butter or margarine
2 tablespoons vinegar
2 tablespoons Worcestershire sauce
1 tablespoon lemon juice
1 (3- to 3½-pound) chicken, cut up

Combine first 12 ingredients in a medium saucepan. Bring to a boil; remove from heat. Dip chicken in barbecue sauce, and place in a large, well-greased, brown bag. Pour remaining sauce over chicken. Close bag; secure with staples.

Place bag in a large Dutch oven; bake, covered, at 500° for 15 minutes. Reduce heat to 300°, and bake 1 hour and 15 minutes. Yield: 4 servings.

OVEN-BARBECUED CHICKEN

1 (3- to 3½-pound) broiler-fryer, cut up
2 tablespoons shortening
2 tablespoons brown sugar
1 tablespoon salt
⅛ teaspoon red pepper
1 medium onion, chopped
½ cup chopped celery
1 cup water
1 cup catsup
¼ cup lemon juice
3 tablespoons Worcestershire sauce
1½ teaspoons prepared mustard

Brown chicken in shortening in an ovenproof Dutch oven over medium heat. Combine next 10 ingredients, mixing well; pour sauce over chicken. Cover and simmer 30 minutes. Uncover; transfer to oven, and bake at 350° for 35 minutes. Yield: 4 servings.

McIlhenny Company, Avery Island, Louisiana

Hot sauce: As essential for barbecue now as then.

BASIC BARBECUED CHICKEN

1 cup vegetable oil
½ cup vinegar
⅛ teaspoon paprika
½ teaspoon salt
¼ teaspoon pepper
1 (3½- to 4-pound) broiler-fryer, quartered

Combine first 5 ingredients; stir well. Place chicken, skin side down, on grill. Grill over medium coals 50 to 60 minutes or until tender, turning chicken every 10 minutes. Brush with sauce during last 20 minutes. Yield: 4 servings.

SPICY GRILLED CHICKEN

3 (2- to 2½-pound) broiler-fryers, quartered
1948 Original Barbecue Sauce

Place chicken, skin side down, on grill, and brown about 10 minutes. Turn chicken, skin side up, and repeat procedure.

Brush chicken with barbecue sauce, and cook over medium coals 25 to 30 minutes. Turn chicken, and brush with sauce about every 10 minutes. Yield: 10 to 12 servings.

1948 Original Barbecue Sauce:

1 medium onion, chopped
2 cloves garlic, minced
2 tablespoons butter or margarine, melted
1 (14½-ounce) can whole tomatoes
1 (8-ounce) can tomato sauce
½ cup chopped celery
¼ cup chopped green pepper
2 fresh celery leaves, chopped
1 bay leaf
3 tablespoons molasses
2 teaspoons dry mustard
2 teaspoons hot sauce
1½ teaspoons salt
⅓ cup vinegar
½ teaspoon ground cloves
½ teaspoon ground allspice
2 lemon slices

Sauté onion and garlic in butter until tender. Stir in remaining ingredients; simmer, uncovered, 30 minutes. Remove from heat, and press mixture through a food mill, if desired. Use to baste chicken when grilling. Yield: about 3 cups.

Both Louisiana and Texas claim credit for originating barbecue. The Cajuns say the word barbecue is from the French *barbe à queue* (from whiskers to tail). Texans are just as sure that the Spanish settlers there picked it up from the Carib Indians who smoke-cooked fish and game on a green wood lattice over fire or hot stones, a process called boucan. The Spanish renamed it *barbacoa*, which became barbecue.

Grilled Chicken and Savory Barbecued Chicken: Mmmm.

MARINATED GRILLED CHICKEN

½ cup butter or margarine
1 cup garlic-flavored wine vinegar
¼ cup Worcestershire sauce
4 drops hot sauce
1 small onion, finely chopped
1 tablespoon sugar
1 teaspoon dry mustard
1 teaspoon salt
1 (3- to 3½-pound) broiler-fryer, quartered

Melt butter in a heavy saucepan. Add next 7 ingredients; bring to a boil, stirring vigorously. Pour sauce over chicken; cover, and marinate at least 4 hours in refrigerator.

Place chicken, skin side down, on grill over medium coals; reserve sauce. Grill 12 minutes; turn skin side up, and cook 12 minutes. Brush chicken with reserved sauce; grill an additional 40 minutes, basting and turning every 10 minutes. Yield: 4 servings.

SAVORY BARBECUED CHICKEN

1½ cups catsup
2 tablespoons prepared mustard
1⅓ cups pickle relish, drained
¼ cup soy sauce
¼ cup firmly packed brown sugar
2 cloves garlic, minced
¼ teaspoon pepper
2 (3- to 3½-pound) broiler-fryer, cut up

Combine catsup and mustard, stirring well. Add next 5 ingredients, mixing thoroughly.
Place chicken, skin side down, on grill. Grill over medium coals 1 hour or until tender, turning chicken every 10 minutes. Brush with sauce during last 25 minutes. Yield: 8 servings.

LEMON-BARBECUED TURKEY

4 small cloves garlic, crushed
2 teaspoons salt
1¾ cups lemon juice
1 cup vegetable oil
½ cup chopped onion
2 teaspoons ground thyme
2 teaspoons pepper
1 (10- to 10½-pound) turkey, quartered

Combine garlic and salt, stirring to blend. Add next 5 ingredients; mix well. Pour sauce over turkey; cover, and marinate overnight in refrigerator.

Place turkey, skin side down, on grill; reserve marinating sauce. Cover, and grill over medium coals 2 hours, turning turkey every 15 minutes. Brush with reserved sauce during last 30 minutes of grilling. Yield: 10 to 12 servings.

Back in the late 1920s, folks went straight to their nearest Ford car dealer for briquettes. Here's why. It was Henry Ford who invented the briquette. In 1924, finding his car factory was a mess with sawdust and wood scraps, Ford decided to burn the trash. The result was powdery charcoal.

It did not take Ford very long to realize that in disposing of industrial waste, he was mass-producing a useful energy source. Then it hit him. He had the powder pressed into uniform little cakes for shipping. And Ford dealers across the country were among the first purveyors of the new product.

SPECIALTIES OF THE HOUSE

Scalloped, Sherried, and All Dolled Up

The transition from plain to fancy fowl can be as subtle as adding a dash of lemon and a pinch of sugar to broiled chicken. Or it can be as overwhelmingly elegant as Turkey au Rochambeau Sauce. In this chapter we leave off the plainer forms of frying, stewing, and roasting to take up some of the fancier ways with fowl of which the South is so fond . . . and so capable.

One exquisite menu from the unique Hermann-Grima House in New Orleans serves to set the tone for the delights to follow. From every possible source have tumbled near-forgotten recipes that reflect differing facets of our history. For the early East Coasters, the combination of chicken with oysters was the most natural thing in the world, closely followed by chicken with ham.

To the Southwest, the Mexican influence gave emphasis to spiciness and to a flavor that still arouses dismay in some who have not tried it: chocolate used as a condiment, as in Chicken Mole. Hungarian immigrants could not keep to themselves their chicken reddened with sweet paprika. The Spanish and French combined forces to make us aware of Creole cooking, while the Acadians further west in Louisiana gave us yet another version of French dishes altered to make use of the native ingredients.

Chicken, of course, is not the whole story on fowl. Squab, always liked in England, has its supporters, but it appears that the guinea fowl has all but disappeared from Southern tables. Unlike geese, which are still valued for their "watchdogging" noisemaking, the guinea's squawking is so incessant and unpleasant that more than one poultryman just gave up on the bird. Breast of chicken and turkey are versatile foundations for the cook's imagination. And the duck has kept a place in Southern cuisine, even though domestic duck is a poor substitute for the game bird to those persons whose ancestors were hunters.

Whether the inspiration of a creative chef or a Southern hostess, these are the recipes you will turn to when you entertain in the grand manner. Subtly refined or smashingly flamboyant, there is a dish for every mood and occasion.

Photographed in splendor at historic Hermann-Grima House, a Victorian meal: Chicken Coliseum (front), Broiled Tomatoes (left), and Poached Pears Julianne with Apricot Sauce (center), ornamented with swans carved from apples.

HERMANN-GRIMA HOSPITALITY

Fireplace and hearth dominate kitchen at Hermann-Grima House. Oven at right.

Menus such as this one could have been, and were, produced in the Hermann-Grima kitchen after 1831, although no one has ever said it was easy . . . even if one had servants and time cooperating. Fascinating as this delicious dinner is, two facts are of special interest.

The first has to do with the mandatory New Orleans roux. For the oyster soup, the roux (mixture of fat and flour) is lightly browned after combining, whereas for the chicken sauce, the flour is dry-browned in a skillet first. Both methods are valid.

Then note that two of the menu elements, the bread (our menu calls for rusks) and the custard, are baked. The order of baking in the brick oven, once it was heated by fire, then raked and mopped out clean, was strict. The bread, needing the highest temperature, would have been baked first. Then any pudding, pastry, cake, and gingerbread. The custard, needing the lowest heat, was baked last. As baking was usually carried out only one day a week, one suspects that a company dinner was planned to coincide as closely as possible with baking day.

OYSTER SOUP À LA NEW ORLEANS
CHICKEN COLISEUM
BROILED TOMATOES
LETTUCE SALAD
WITH OIL AND VINEGAR DRESSING
POACHED PEARS JULIANNE
or
BAKED CUSTARD WITH RUM SAUCE

Serves 8

OYSTER SOUP À LA NEW ORLEANS

1½ teaspoons vegetable oil
1½ teaspoons butter or
    margarine
1 tablespoon flour
1½ cups finely chopped
    celery
3 green onions, chopped
2 (12-ounce) containers fresh
    Select oysters, undrained
3 cups boiling water
1 cup milk, scalded
¾ teaspoon salt
⅛ teaspoon pepper
2 teaspoons finely chopped
    fresh parsley

Combine oil and butter in a large Dutch oven; cook over low heat, stirring until butter melts. Add flour, stirring until smooth. Cook over low heat 1 minute, stirring constantly.

Add celery and onion to Dutch oven; cook 10 minutes or until vegetables are tender. Stir in oysters and liquid; cook an additional 10 minutes. Gradually add water; cook over medium heat 30 minutes. Stir in milk, salt, pepper, and parsley. Serve hot. Yield: about 10 cups.

BROILED TOMATOES

8 medium tomatoes
2 tablespoons plus 2
    teaspoons butter or
    margarine
¼ teaspoon salt
⅛ teaspoon pepper
¼ cup grated Parmesan
    cheese

Remove stems from tomatoes. Cut a ¼-inch slice from top of each. Place 1 teaspoon butter on top of each tomato; sprinkle with salt, pepper, and cheese. Broil 5 minutes, 4 inches from heat. Yield: 8 servings.

CHICKEN COLISEUM

1 cup all-purpose flour
1 teaspoon salt
½ teaspoon pepper
4 whole chicken breasts,
    split, boned, and skinned
Vegetable oil
½ cup all-purpose flour
½ cup butter or margarine
⅔ cup chicken broth
⅔ cup Chablis or other dry
    white wine
16 pearl onions, peeled
⅔ cup diagonally sliced
    carrots
1 pound fresh mushrooms,
    sliced
½ teaspoon salt
¼ teaspoon pepper
5 drops hot sauce
16 cherry tomatoes
16 fresh brussels sprouts
⅓ cup brandy
8 Holland Rusk biscuits
⅓ cup chopped fresh parsley

Combine first 3 ingredients in a plastic or paper bag; shake to mix. Place 2 or 3 pieces of chicken in bag; shake well. Repeat procedure with remaining chicken.

Heat 1 inch of oil to 325° in a large skillet; add chicken, and cook 15 minutes or until golden brown, turning occasionally. Drain on paper towels, and set chicken aside.

Place ½ cup flour in a small skillet; cook over low heat, stirring constantly, until flour is browned.

Melt butter in a Dutch oven over low heat; add browned flour, stirring until smooth. Cook 1 minute, stirring constantly. Gradually add broth and wine; cook over medium heat, stirring constantly, 15 minutes or until thickened and bubbly.

Add chicken, onions, carrots, mushrooms, salt, pepper, and hot sauce to white sauce in Dutch oven; mix well. Cover, and cook over low heat 20 minutes. Add tomatoes and brussels sprouts, mixing well. Continue cooking, covered, an additional 15 minutes. Stir in brandy, and simmer 10 minutes. Spoon chicken mixture over Holland Rusk biscuits, and garnish with chopped parsley. Yield: 8 servings.

POACHED PEARS JULIANNE

8 medium pears
4 cups water
1 cup sugar
1 tablespoon lemon juice
¾ cup apricot preserves

Peel pears, removing core from bottom end; leave stems intact. Slice about ¼ inch from bottom of each pear to make a flat base. Set pears aside.

Combine water, sugar, and lemon juice in a 5-quart Dutch oven; bring to a boil over medium heat, stirring until sugar dissolves. Place pears in Dutch oven in an upright position. Cover and simmer 20 minutes (straighten pears if they tilt while cooking).

Using a slotted spoon, transfer pears to a 10- x 6- x 2-inch baking dish. Heat apricot preserves over low heat in a small saucepan; strain, and pour sauce over pears; cover and refrigerate until thoroughly chilled. Yield: 8 servings.

The restored Hermann-Grima House, a National Historic Landmark.

BAKED CUSTARD WITH RUM SAUCE

5 eggs, slightly beaten
½ cup plus 3 tablespoons
 sugar
¼ teaspoon salt
4 cups milk, scalded
2 teaspoons vanilla extract
Ground nutmeg
Rum Sauce

Combine first 3 ingredients, beating well; gradually add milk, stirring constantly. Stir in vanilla. Pour into eight 6-ounce custard cups. Sprinkle with nutmeg.

Place custard cups in a 13- x 9- x 2-inch baking dish; pour hot water into pan to a depth of 1½ inches. Bake at 325° for 50 minutes or until knife inserted halfway between center and edge of custard cup comes out clean. Remove cups from water; cool. Unmold and serve with Rum Sauce. Yield: 8 servings.

Rum Sauce:

2 eggs, slightly beaten
3 tablespoons sugar
⅛ teaspoon salt
1⅓ cups milk, scalded
1½ teaspoons rum extract
¼ teaspoon ground nutmeg

Combine eggs, sugar, and salt in a heavy saucepan; gradually stir in milk. Cook over low heat, stirring constantly, until mixture is thickened and bubbly and coats a metal spoon. Remove from heat; cool slightly. Stir in rum extract and nutmeg. Spoon over baked custard. Yield: 2 cups.

In December 1831, Samuel Hermann, Sr., saw his new house at 820 St. Louis Street in New Orleans completed. Adjacent to it was a new kitchen containing the latest in cooking equipment. In addition to an open-hearth oven, a brick baking oven, and a tin kitchen, there was a masonry counter-topped "stew-hole" or potager with four places for cooking utensils. The Ursuline Convent kitchen, built in 1745, had eleven openings in its potager, but for a private home, these four were adequate.

WINNING ENTRÉES

CAVATONI CHICKEN EGGPLANT FRANCESCA

3 whole chicken breasts, split, boned, and skinned
1 cup all-purpose flour
1 teaspoon salt
¼ teaspoon pepper
¼ cup olive oil
Red Gravy Sauce
1 medium eggplant, peeled and cut into ½-inch-thick slices
1 (12-ounce) package vermicelli
1 cup sliced fresh mushrooms
1 (12-ounce) package mozzarella cheese, thinly sliced

Place each chicken breast half on waxed paper; flatten to ¼-inch thickness using a meat mallet or rolling pin.

Combine flour, salt, and pepper in a plastic or paper bag; shake to mix. Place 2 or 3 pieces of chicken in bag; shake well. Repeat procedure with remaining chicken.

Heat oil in a large skillet. Add chicken; sauté over medium heat 7 minutes on each side or until golden brown. Drain; reserve oil in skillet. Marinate chicken in Red Gravy Sauce 10 minutes.

Sauté eggplant in reserved oil until golden brown on both sides; drain and set aside.

Cook vermicelli according to package directions; drain. Spoon into a lightly greased 13-x 9- x 2-inch baking dish. Sprinkle mushrooms evenly over vermicelli. Place chicken breasts over mushrooms, and cover with sauce. Top with eggplant and cheese slices. Bake at 375° for 15 minutes or until cheese melts and sauce is bubbly. Yield: 6 servings.

Fresh vegetables enhance the elegant Cavatoni Chicken Eggplant Francesca.

Red Gravy Sauce:
1 cup chopped green pepper
1 cup chopped onion
½ cup chopped green onion
3 cloves garlic, minced
⅓ cup vegetable oil
1 (10¾-ounce) can tomato puree
1 cup sliced fresh mushrooms
1 bay leaf

1 cup sherry
1 teaspoon salt
⅛ teaspoon pepper

Sauté green pepper, onion, and garlic in oil in a medium saucepan until tender. Add tomato puree, mushrooms, and bay leaf; simmer 25 minutes. Stir in sherry, salt, and pepper; continue cooking 5 minutes. Remove bay leaf. Yield: about 4½ cups.

The Homestead in Virginia, long famous for its food.

BROILED CHICKEN DELUXE

1 (3- to 3½-pound)
    broiler-fryer, split
1 lemon, halved
2 teaspoons salt
¼ teaspoon pepper
½ teaspoon paprika
½ cup butter or margarine,
    melted and divided
2 teaspoons sugar

Place chicken, breast side up, in a shallow roasting pan. Rub entire surface of chicken halves with lemon, squeezing out juice occasionally. Combine salt, pepper, and paprika; sprinkle over chicken. Brush chicken with ¼ cup butter; sprinkle with sugar. Bake, uncovered, at 450° for 10 minutes. Baste with remaining butter. Reduce heat to 350°; cover and bake an additional 35 minutes or until tender. Yield: 4 servings.

Their winning ways have earned this block of recipes a chapter of their own. Some have won prizes for their creators; others have been tested for generations in famous hostelries such as The Homestead in Virginia, winning applause with every plateful. Then there are the old timers that have just always been here; with such staying power, they'll never be dropped from Southern menus.

Back in 1949, Edna Selkirk of Salisbury, Maryland, won first prize when the first National Chicken Cooking Contest was held. Her Broiled Chicken Deluxe is an object lesson: it does not require dozens of ingredients to bring forth a splendid chicken dish, just imagination and care.

We must take care not to lose other Southern treasures like the Escalloped Chicken bequeathed to us by the Frances Virginia Tearoom, that genteel oasis that was a Peachtree Street landmark in Atlanta for so long. Cavatoni Chicken Eggplant Francesca, from Pascal's Manale in New Orleans, gaudily sauced, fits as neatly into our "Winning Entrees" as does the 200-year old Maryland recipe for Chicken with Oyster Sauce. They prove the timelessness of the South's devotion to fancy fowl.

THE HOMESTEAD FRIED CHICKEN

¼ cup all-purpose flour
1 teaspoon salt
¼ teaspoon pepper
1 cup plus 2 tablespoons
   half-and-half, divided
4 whole chicken breasts,
   split, boned, and skinned
½ cup butter or margarine,
   melted
3 medium-size sweet
   potatoes, cooked, pared, and
   sliced
¾ cup firmly packed brown
   sugar
1½ tablespoons lemon juice
¼ teaspoon salt
2 tablespoons butter or
   margarine
2 medium bananas, sliced
1 tablespoon all-purpose flour
1 tablespoon maple syrup
8 hot cooked waffles
8 slices hot cooked country
   ham

Combine first 3 ingredients; mix well, and set aside.

Sprinkle 2 tablespoons half-and-half evenly over chicken breasts; dredge in flour mixture. Place 4 chicken breast halves in ½ cup melted butter in a large skillet; cook over medium heat 3 to 4 minutes on each side or until golden brown. Repeat procedure with remaining chicken breast halves. Reserve pan drippings in skillet. Place chicken in a lightly greased 13- x 9- x 2-inch baking dish. Bake, uncovered, at 325° for 30 minutes.

Place sweet potatoes in a 13- x 9- x 2-inch baking dish. Sprinkle with sugar, lemon juice, and salt. Dot with 2 tablespoons butter. Bake, uncovered, at 375° for 20 minutes. Stir in bananas.

Add 1 tablespoon flour to reserved drippings in skillet; stir until smooth. Cook 1 minute, stirring constantly. Gradually add remaining 1 cup half-and-half and syrup; cook over medium heat, stirring constantly, until thickened and bubbly.

Arrange waffles on a platter. Top each with a ham slice, a chicken breast half, and candied sweet potatoes and bananas. Serve with sauce. Yield: 8 servings.

The Homestead Fried Chicken keeps people coming back.

Wooden butter mold, 1800.

ESCALLOPED CHICKEN, GEORGIA-STYLE

2 cups sliced fresh
   mushrooms
1 tablespoon finely chopped
   onion
3 tablespoons butter or
   margarine
¼ cup all-purpose flour
1½ cups chicken broth
½ cup milk
2 cups cubed cooked
   chicken
2 cups cooked rice
¼ cup plus 2 tablespoons
   sliced almonds
2 tablespoons chopped
   pimiento
½ teaspoon salt
¼ teaspoon pepper
4 slices bread, toasted and
   crumbled
¼ cup plus 2 tablespoons
   butter or margarine, melted
½ teaspoon paprika

Sauté mushrooms and onion in butter in a large skillet until tender. Stir in flour. Gradually add broth and milk, stirring until smooth. Cook over medium heat, stirring constantly, until thickened and bubbly. Remove from heat. Stir in chicken, rice, almonds, pimiento, salt, and pepper. Spoon into a lightly greased 2-quart casserole. Top with breadcrumbs. Pour butter over crumbs, and sprinkle with paprika. Bake at 350° for 20 minutes or until lightly browned. Yield: 6 servings.

A late nineteenth-century label for the "Triangle" brand Baltimore oysters.

Staples & Charles

OYSTER-STUFFED BREAST OF CHICKEN

1 (12-ounce) container fresh
   Select oysters, drained and
   chopped
3 tablespoons chopped green
   pepper
3 tablespoons chopped fresh
   parsley
2 tablespoons chopped celery
2 tablespoons chopped onion
1 clove garlic, crushed
1 teaspoon salt
¼ teaspoon coarsely ground
   black pepper
¼ teaspoon red pepper
¼ cup butter or margarine
2 whole chicken breasts, split
1 tablespoon butter or
   margarine, melted
½ cup water
⅓ cup soft breadcrumbs
1 tablespoon plus 1 teaspoon
   butter or margarine

Combine first 9 ingredients in a medium-size skillet; sauté in ¼ cup butter until tender, and set aside. Place chicken, breast side up, in a 12- x 8- x 2-inch baking dish; brush with 1 tablespoon melted butter. Pour water into baking dish; bake, uncovered, at 375° for 30 minutes or until lightly browned.

Remove from oven, and turn chicken breasts cavity side up. Fill each cavity with about ¼ cup sautéed oyster mixture. Sprinkle with breadcrumbs, and dot with remaining butter. Return to oven, and bake an additional 20 minutes or until golden brown. Yield: 4 servings.

Collection
of Business
Americana

CHICKEN WITH OYSTER SAUCE

1 (3- to 3½-pound)
   broiler-fryer, quartered
3 tablespoons butter or
   margarine
1 cup whipping cream
¼ teaspoon salt
⅛ teaspoon pepper
¼ cup all-purpose flour
1 (12-ounce) container fresh
   Select oysters, drained and
   coarsely chopped

Brown chicken in butter in a large skillet. Transfer to a 13- x 9- x 2-inch baking dish. Cover and bake at 375° for 30 minutes. Add cream, salt, and pepper to baking dish. Cover, and bake an additional 30 minutes or until chicken is tender. Remove chicken; place on a serving platter, and keep warm. Reserve pan juices.

Pour ¾ cup of juices into a saucepan, and place over low heat. Add flour, stirring until smooth. Cook 1 minute, stirring constantly. Gradually add remaining reserved juices and oysters; cook over medium heat, stirring constantly, until thickened and bubbly. Spoon sauce over chicken. Yield: 4 servings.

CHICKEN PICCATA

4 whole chicken breasts,
   split, boned, and
   skinned
1 tablespoon butter or
   margarine, melted
2 tablespoons olive oil
¼ cup lemon juice
½ teaspoon salt
⅛ teaspoon pepper
1 tablespoon butter or
   margarine, melted

Place each chicken breast half
on a sheet of waxed paper; flatten to ¼-inch thickness, using a
meat mallet or rolling pin.

Lightly brown chicken in 1 tablespoon butter and oil in a
large skillet over low heat. Remove chicken to a warmed serving platter, reserving pan
drippings in skillet. Add lemon
juice, salt, and pepper to skillet.
Cook over medium heat, stirring constantly, until thickened
and bubbly. Stir in 1 tablespoon
melted butter. Spoon sauce over
chicken. Yield: 4 servings.

*Rooster motif in
a hand-hooked rug,
c.1850.*

CHICKEN SAUTÉ,
MEXICAINE

1 (3½- to 4-pound)
   broiler-fryer, cut up
½ teaspoon salt
¼ cup butter or margarine
1 medium onion, chopped
2 medium-size green peppers,
   chopped
3 medium tomatoes, peeled
   and quartered
12 medium-size fresh
   mushrooms, sliced
¼ cup Chablis or other dry
   white wine
1 to 2 tablespoons seeded,
   chopped jalapeño peppers
½ to 1 teaspoon hot sauce
Hot cooked rice

Sprinkle chicken with salt.
Melt butter in a large Dutch
oven; add chicken, and brown
on all sides. Remove chicken,
and set aside.

Add onion and green pepper
to drippings in Dutch oven;
sauté until tender. Add next 5
ingredients, stirring well. Return chicken to Dutch oven,
and cook, uncovered, over low
heat 45 minutes or until
chicken is tender. Serve chicken
with rice. Yield: 4 servings.

SHERRIED CORNISH
HENS

4 (1¼-pound) Cornish hens,
   split
1 tablespoon lemon juice
2 teaspoons salt
1 teaspoon pepper
½ cup butter or margarine,
   melted
½ cup sherry
2 tablespoons all-purpose
   flour
1 (8-ounce) can sliced
   mushrooms, drained

Rinse hens with cold water,
and pat dry. Combine lemon
juice, salt, and pepper; rub mixture over hens. Place hens,
breast side up, in a shallow
roasting pan. Brush with butter; pour sherry over hens.
Cover lightly, and bake at 325°
for 1 hour. Uncover and broil 6
inches from heat about 10 minutes. Transfer hens to a large
serving platter; set aside.

Combine pan drippings and
flour in a skillet, stirring until
smooth. Cook over medium
heat, stirring constantly, until
thickened and bubbly. Stir in
mushrooms. Spoon gravy over
hens. Yield: 4 servings.

99

Chef Fred Crawford served as the Executive Chef at the Williamsburg Inn for thirty-four years, after being hired by the Rockefellers in 1937. While at Williamsburg, he prepared banquets for such royal personages and dignitaries as Queen Elizabeth and Prince Phillip, Sir Winston and Lady Churchill, Cardinal Spellman, and the King and Queen of Greece. He also served his special dishes to our presidents: Franklin D. Roosevelt, Harry S. Truman, and Dwight D. Eisenhower.

In 1947, Chef Crawford carried off top honors at the Chefs' Tournament held at Virginia Beach, a competition sponsored by the Virginia State Chamber of Commerce. For this Tournament, all competitors were to prepare a full dinner. Chef Crawford chose to feature as his entree the Breast of Turkey Supreme, as winsome today as when Crawford presented it to the judges who themselves were some of the country's leading epicures.

Mrs. Big Onion;—"You are so small you make me weep!"

CHEF CRAWFORD'S BREAST OF TURKEY SUPREME

½ cup butter or margarine
½ cup all-purpose flour
1 cup chicken broth
½ cup milk
½ cup whipping cream
½ teaspoon salt
¼ teaspoon white pepper
4 cups hot cooked rice
1 pound sliced smoked turkey breast
½ cup sliced almonds, toasted

Melt butter in a heavy saucepan over low heat; add flour, stirring until smooth. Cook 1 minute, stirring constantly. Gradually add broth, milk, and cream; cook over medium heat, stirring constantly, until thickened and bubbly. Stir in salt and pepper; reduce heat, and cook an additional 10 minutes, stirring constantly.

Place ½ cup rice on individual serving plates. Spoon cream sauce over rice; arrange turkey slices over rice. Top with remaining cream sauce. Sprinkle with almonds. Yield: 8 servings.

ROSY DUCKLING

2 cloves garlic, crushed
1 teaspoon minced onion
½ teaspoon celery salt
½ teaspoon salt
1 (4½- to 5-pound) duckling, quartered
3 tablespoons all-purpose flour
1 (16-ounce) can whole-berry cranberry sauce
Additional cranberry sauce

Combine garlic, onion, celery salt, and salt; rub mixture over duckling. Roll duckling quarters in flour; place skin side up in a 13- x 9- x 2-inch baking dish. Spoon cranberry sauce on top; cover and bake at 325° for 2½ hours or until tender. Remove duckling from baking dish; drain well, and transfer to serving platter. Serve with cranberry sauce. Yield: 4 servings.

A PLACE IN HISTORY

CHICKEN À LA MARENGO

1 (2½- to 3-pound)
   broiler-fryer, cut up
¼ cup olive oil
1 (6-ounce) can button
   mushrooms, drained
1 clove garlic, minced
1 teaspoon chopped fresh
   parsley
1 large tomato, finely chopped
3 tablespoons lemon juice
½ teaspoon salt
¼ teaspoon pepper

Brown chicken on all sides in hot oil in a large skillet. Add remaining ingredients, stirring well. Reduce heat, and cook, covered, 1 hour or until chicken is tender. Yield: 4 servings.

CHICKEN MARENGO

2 (2½- to 3-pound)
   broiler-fryers, cut up
¼ cup olive oil
1 medium onion, sliced
1 pound fresh mushrooms,
   sliced
½ cup Chablis or other dry
   white wine
1 can beef bouillon
1 (16-ounce) can stewed
   tomatoes
1 tablespoon chopped fresh
   parsley
1 bay leaf
½ teaspoon thyme
Salt and pepper to taste
2 tablespoons flour
¼ cup sliced pimiento-stuffed
   olives

Brown chicken in hot oil in a large skillet; drain, and transfer to a 13- x 9- x 2-inch baking dish. Reserve drippings in skillet. Sauté onion and mushrooms in drippings until tender. Add next 8 ingredients; mix well. Cook over medium heat 5 minutes. Add olives, and mix well. Remove bay leaf.
Pour mixture over chicken. Cover, and bake at 350° for 45 minutes or until chicken is tender. Yield: 8 servings.

C hicken Marengo was one of Thomas Jefferson's recipes from France, but it was probably not close to the original. The dish was invented by Napoleon's chef to celebrate his victory over the Austrians at Marengo in the Italian Piedmont in 1800. The valiant chef liberated some chickens and all the rich Italian produce he needed: olive oil, tomatoes (it was summer), garlic, and wine. If his armies marched on their stomachs, then Napoleon out-marched them all; he had a chef who knew how to treat him.

Chicken à la Marengo. Based on a recipe from Napoleonic era.

Captains in Surinam, *by John Greenwood, c.1760, imaginatively depicts the life of the spice trader.*

COUNTRY CAPTAIN

½ cup all-purpose flour
2 teaspoons salt, divided
½ teaspoon pepper
1 (3- to 3½-pound)
    broiler-fryer, cut up and
    skinned
½ cup lard
2 medium onions, chopped
2 medium-size green peppers,
    chopped
1 clove garlic, minced
2 (14½-ounce) cans whole
    tomatoes, undrained and
    chopped
1 tablespoon chopped fresh
    parsley
2 teaspoons curry powder
½ teaspoon white pepper
½ teaspoon ground thyme
2 cups hot cooked rice
¾ cup currants
1 cup slivered almonds,
    toasted
Fresh parsley sprigs
Chutney

Combine flour, 1 teaspoon salt, and pepper, and mix well. Dredge chicken pieces in flour mixture. Heat lard in a heavy skillet. Brown chicken on all sides, and transfer to a 13- x 9- x 2-inch baking dish, reserving pan drippings.

Add onion, green pepper, and garlic to pan drippings; sauté until tender. Add tomatoes, parsley, curry powder, white pepper, thyme, and remaining salt; stir well, and pour over chicken. Cover and bake at 350° for 45 minutes or until chicken is tender. Remove chicken to a serving platter, reserving sauce; spoon rice around chicken. Add currants to sauce mixture; stir well. Pour sauce over rice. Sprinkle with almonds, and garnish with parsley. Serve chutney as an accompaniment. Yield: 6 servings.

In order to place some of our Southern classic chicken dishes into perspective, let's do a bit of poking into the past. For example, an occasional visitor from outside the South will express disbelief that curry could be an ingredient in our traditional Country Captain. It would be stranger still if we had not had it for so long. Curry ingredients figured large in the spice trade even before the seventeenth century when the British and Dutch East India companies were formed. The pretty stories surrounding the introduction of curry may all be true, or none of them. The fact remains that the many separate spices that comprise curry should have arrived here within a very few years after the East Coast had been settled.

CURRIED CHICKEN

1 (3½- to 4-pound)
  broiler-fryer, cut up
1 teaspoon salt
½ cup butter or margarine
1 medium onion, chopped
1 stalk celery, chopped
2 small cloves garlic, minced
1 Granny Smith apple, cored
  and finely chopped
¼ pound cooked ham,
  chopped
1 small bay leaf
¼ teaspoon dry mustard
2 tablespoons all-purpose
  flour
2 teaspoons curry powder
½ teaspoon ground mace
½ cup coconut juice
1 cup whipping cream
Hot cooked rice
Condiments

Place chicken, salt, and water to cover in a Dutch oven. Bring to a boil; reduce heat, and simmer 1 hour or until tender. Remove chicken from broth, reserving 2 cups broth; cool. Bone chicken, and cut into bite-size pieces. Set aside.

Melt butter in a heavy skillet over low heat; add next 7 ingredients, and mix well. Cook over medium heat 8 minutes. Stir in flour, curry powder, and mace; cook an additional 4 minutes. Gradually add reserved chicken broth and coconut juice. Simmer over low heat 1 hour; strain. Reserve curry sauce; discard vegetable-ham mixture. Stir cream and chicken into curry sauce; cook over medium heat 10 minutes. Serve over rice with several of the following condiments: (about 1 cup each) chutney, flaked coconut, chopped hard-cooked egg, crumbled cooked bacon, salted peanuts, and chopped green onion. Yield: 6 servings.

Curried Chicken also takes to other exotic condiments: shredded dried shrimp, toasted almonds, "Bombay duck" (dried jellyfish), candied ginger, chopped banana....

Curry is so widely used in the East that it is known as the "salt of the Orient." In India, the cook prepares curry daily from fresh ingredients, making it either in paste or powder form. Tamarind is the basic spice in curry paste, and turmeric the foundation of powdered curry. Fenugreek, coriander, ginger, caraway, various peppers, and other spices are also part of the powder. A purist will look down his nose at our bottle labeled "curry powder" and say that true curry cannot be made ouside India and without fresh ingredients. A fair substitute may be composed by starting with green chiles and fresh ginger and mixing in dried spices until the right balance between insipid and unbearable is obtained. A true curry lover may well enjoy experimenting; there are books available on the subject.

Chicken Divan: A Southern luncheon favorite.

CHICKEN DIVAN

¼ cup plus 2 tablespoons
  butter or margarine, divided
2 whole chicken breasts,
  split, boned, and skinned
½ cup water
3 green onions, finely
  chopped
2 tablespoons all-purpose
  flour
½ teaspoon salt
¼ teaspoon pepper
1 cup half-and-half
¼ cup dry white wine
¼ cup grated Parmesan
  cheese, divided
1½ pounds fresh asparagus
  spears, cooked

Melt 3 tablespoons butter in a large skillet; brown chicken in butter on all sides. Add water; cover, and cook over low heat 15 minutes or until chicken is tender. Set aside.

Melt remaining butter in a small saucepan; add onion, and sauté 2 minutes. Stir in flour, salt, and pepper. Gradually add half-and-half and wine; cook over medium heat, stirring constantly, until thickened and bubbly. Stir in 2 tablespoons Parmesan cheese.

Arrange asparagus spears in 4 equal portions in a lightly greased 13- x 9- x 2-inch baking dish.

Place a chicken breast half on each portion of asparagus spears. Spoon sauce over chicken. Top with remaining cheese. Bake at 350° for 15 minutes or until lightly browned. Yield: 4 servings.

MARYLAND CHICKEN AND COUNTRY HAM

1 (3- to 3½-pound)
  broiler-fryer, quartered
1 medium onion
2 cloves garlic
2 stalks celery
3 or 4 sprigs fresh parsley
1 teaspoon salt
2 cups soft breadcrumbs
1 small onion, minced
2 tablespoons chopped fresh
  parsley
1 teaspoon dried whole
  savory
Dash of pepper
6 thin slices lean country
  ham
2 tablespoons butter or
  margarine
2 tablespoons all-purpose
  flour
1 cup half-and-half
Dash of ground nutmeg

Combine first 6 ingredients and water to cover in a Dutch oven; bring to a boil. Cover; reduce heat, and simmer 1 hour or until chicken is tender. Remove chicken from broth; cool. Strain broth, reserving ⅔ cup. Discard vegetables. Bone chicken, and chop meat. Place chopped chicken in a 12- x 8- x 2-inch baking dish.

Combine breadcrumbs, onion, chopped parsley, savory, and pepper in a small mixing bowl. Stir in reserved broth; mix well. Set aside 3 tablespoons stuffing mixture. Spoon remaining stuffing in center of each slice of ham, and roll up tightly. Arrange ham rolls, seam side down, around chicken in baking dish.

Melt butter in a heavy saucepan over low heat; add flour, stirring until smooth. Cook 1 minute, stirring constantly. Gradually add half-and-half; cook over medium heat, stirring constantly, until thickened and bubbly. Stir in nutmeg. Spoon sauce over chicken and ham rolls; sprinkle with reserved stuffing. Bake, covered, at 350° for 15 minutes. Uncover, and bake an additional 15 minutes. Yield: 6 to 8 servings.

EDWARDS HOUSE CHICKEN

½ cup all-purpose flour
1 teaspoon salt
½ teaspoon pepper
1 (3½- to 4-pound)
  broiler-fryer, cut up
¼ cup shortening
¼ cup butter or margarine
½ teaspoon dried whole
  thyme
3 small onions, thinly sliced
½ cup butter or margarine,
  melted

Combine flour, salt, and pepper; mix well. Dredge chicken in flour mixture. Heat shortening and butter over medium heat in a heavy skillet. Brown chicken on all sides; transfer chicken to a 13- x 9- x 2-inch baking dish. Sprinkle thyme evenly over chicken; top with onion slices. Pour ¼ cup melted butter over chicken. Bake at 350° for 1 hour, basting with remaining butter every 15 minutes. Yield: 4 to 6 servings.

CHICKEN MOLE

1 (2½- to 3-pound)
  broiler-fryer, cut up and
  skinned
Salt and pepper
¼ cup butter or margarine,
  melted
¼ cup minced onion
¼ cup minced green pepper
1 clove garlic, minced
1 (8¼-ounce) can tomatoes,
  undrained and chopped
½ cup beef broth
2 teaspoons sugar
½ teaspoon chili powder
⅛ teaspoon ground cinnamon
⅛ teaspoon ground nutmeg
Dash of ground cloves
5 to 6 drops hot sauce
¼ (1-ounce) square
  unsweetened chocolate
1 tablespoon cornstarch
2 tablespoon cold water

Sprinkle chicken with salt and pepper; sauté on all sides in melted butter until brown. Remove chicken from skillet, and set aside.

Add onion, green pepper, and garlic to skillet; sauté until tender. Stir in next 9 ingredients; add chicken. Reduce heat, and cook, covered, 45 minutes or until chicken is tender. Remove chicken to serving platter, and keep warm.

Combine cornstarch and water; mix well. Add to sauce in skillet; cook, stirring constantly, until thickened and bubbly. Spoon sauce over chicken. Yield: 4 servings.

Stylized scene of an early Mexican produce market by native artist. Indian crops were just as varied and plentiful in the Southwest as they were on the East Coast, to the surprise and delight of the Europeans who settled there.

CHICKEN PAPRIKA

2 (2½- to 3-pound)
  broiler-fryers, cut up
1¼ cups all-purpose flour,
  divided
Vegetable oil
¼ cup butter or margarine
2 cups milk
2 teaspoons paprika
1 teaspoon salt
¼ teaspoon hot sauce

Dredge chicken in 1 cup flour. Heat oil in a Dutch oven to 375°. Add chicken, and fry 20 min-utes or until golden brown. Drain.

Melt butter in a heavy sauce-pan over low heat; add remaining ¼ cup flour, stirring until smooth. Cook 1 minute, stirring constantly. Gradually add milk; cook over medium heat, stirring constantly, until thickened and bubbly. Stir in paprika, salt, and hot sauce. Place chicken on a serving platter, and spoon sauce over the top. Serve warm. Yield: 8 servings.

The Comte de Rochambeau

COMPOTE OF PIGEONS

4 squabs, split
¾ teaspoon salt, divided
½ teaspoon pepper, divided
3 tablespoons butter or
  margarine
2 tablespoons all-purpose
  flour
2 cups beef broth
½ cup sliced fresh
  mushrooms
1 small onion, sliced
1 bay leaf
2 whole cloves
Toast points
Fresh parsley sprigs

Sprinkle squabs with ½ teaspoon salt and ¼ teaspoon pepper. Melt butter in a skillet; add squabs, and cook until brown. Transfer squabs to a 3-quart casserole, reserving drippings in skillet.

Add flour to pan drippings; stir until smooth. Cook 1 minute, stirring constantly. Gradually add broth; cook over medium heat, stirring constantly, until thickened and bubbly. Stir in remaining salt and pepper. Add mushrooms, onion, bay leaf, and cloves; cook over medium heat, stirring occasionally, until thoroughly heated.

Pour sauce over squabs, and cook, covered, over low heat for 45 minutes or until squabs are tender. Remove bay leaf and cloves; discard. Serve squabs with toast points. Garnish with parsley. Yield: 4 servings.

TURKEY AU ROCHAMBEAU

10 slices smoked turkey
  breast (about 2 pounds)
¼ cup butter or margarine
10 slices cooked ham
10 pineapple slices
10 slices toast
Sauce Rochambeau

Sauté turkey slices in butter in a large skillet for 5 minutes. Place 1 slice turkey, 1 slice ham, and 1 slice pineapple on each slice of toast. Spoon warm Sauce Rochambeau over each sandwich. Yield: 10 open-faced sandwiches.

Sauce Rochambeau:

½ cup butter or margarine
½ cup all-purpose flour
2 cups whipping cream
2 cups (8 ounces) shredded
  Cheddar cheese
½ cup sherry
½ teaspoon salt
¼ teaspoon white pepper

Melt butter in a heavy sauce-pan over low heat; add flour, stirring until smooth. Cook 1 minute, stirring constantly. Gradually add cream; cook over medium heat, stirring constantly, until thickened and bubbly. Add cheese, stirring until cheese melts. Stir in remaining ingredients; cook over medium heat until thickened. Yield: about 2½ cups.

Artist John James Audubon was as impressed by the size and beauty as by the flavor of the wild turkey.

A mong our treasured recipes are those from once-popular eating places that have passed into history. All cities have lost something over the years, yet the fine old hotels are among the saddest of those losses. The Robert E. Lee Hotel in Jackson, Mississippi, featured Turkey au Rochambeau Sauce as specialite de la maison. Jackson also laments the demise of the Edwards House and one of its very special entrees, a tempting "smother" of chicken and onions. Loving memories . . . and recipes . . . remain. All of us know that kind of place. Was the food truly as fine as we remember it? Most likely it was.

FRINGE BENEFITS

Heavenly Hashes and Other Bonuses

———————

L oose ends time has come, just in case you have been scrambling through the chapters looking for hash, liver pâté, or croquettes. Time now to round up all the good things we make from cut-up chicken, from salads to omelets. These small bits of meat are not under any circumstances to be construed as leftovers; we make them on purpose. Well, perhaps you could have enough roast chicken left from dinner to make an omelet, but for those salads, hashes, or creamed dishes that call for several cups of cut-up chicken, "First you cook the chicken!"

It may be worth repeating here that we get richer flavor from mature chickens than from small fryers. To that end, here is Simmered Chicken:

> Place a large hen in a pot that fits it rather closely so that it will not take a flood of water to cover it. Add a small onion with a clove in it, a broken carrot, a handful of celery leaves, a bay leaf, a lemon wedge, a tablespoon of salt, and a dozen peppercorns. Cover and bring to a boil. Lower heat, and barely simmer for as long as it takes chicken to become very tender. Allow to cool for an hour in the broth. Strain and reserve the broth (it freezes well) for soups and sauces; keep the bones, broken and frozen, for gumbo or soup. And, of course, the meat for the recipe in question.

A roast turkey is more generous than chicken when it comes to encore dishes, and quick work should be made of getting the leftover meat wrapped and into the freezer in useable quantities. For Turkey au Gratin, Turkey Soufflé, or Turkey Spoonbread, every scrap is more money in the cook's bank. Sandwiches of chicken or turkey slices can be special, too. Just try the Louisville Hot Brown or the Duke of Windsor Sandwich created by Helen Corbitt in honor of the Duke's visit to Neiman-Marcus' Zodiac Room.

To end on one of the South's inborn traditions, "Waste not, want not," we append a recipe for making a rich stock from the turkey carcass. Store it in quart-size milk cartons in the freezer; it will give you a sense of security.

A drugstore lunch at home: Plate holds Chicken Salad Sandwiches, Tomato Soup, chips, and pickle spears. Snowballs (rear) rolled in coconut are for dessert.

AFTER THE FEAST

"Highland Park Chic" is what they call it in Dallas. That means having lunch on a green plastic-covered stool at the counter in Thell Bowlin's pharmacy. This vintage Texas institution on Knox Street has never stopped doing what so many drugstores used to do: serving up sandwiches with homemade fillings, milkshakes, and malts to a human tide of customers. The clientele are so taken with "their" place that Bowlin is reluctant to change anything for fear of estranging them, although he is the first to admit that the place is looking a tad shabby.

The lunch counter in the corner drugstore has passed almost entirely into history; few exist now except in far-reaching memories. Getting rid of the lunch counter was one way of discouraging loitering, according to some pharmacy owners.

TOMATO SOUP
HIGHLAND PARK
CHICKEN SALAD SANDWICHES
POTATO CHIPS
DILL PICKLE SLICES
SNOWBALLS

Serves 6

TOMATO SOUP

8 medium tomatoes, quartered (about 6 cups)
3 cups water
1 medium onion, chopped
2 small bay leaves
1½ teaspoons celery seeds
1½ teaspoons salt
¼ teaspoon pepper
¼ teaspoon red pepper
¼ cup plus 2 tablespoons butter or margarine, melted
4½ tablespoons all-purpose flour

Combine first 8 ingredients in a Dutch oven, stirring well; bring to a boil. Combine butter and flour, stirring to form a smooth paste. Add flour mixture to tomato mixture, stirring well. Reduce heat; simmer, uncovered, 15 minutes, stirring occasionally. Remove from heat; discard bay leaves. Process mixture through a food mill; discard pulp. Serve soup with crackers. Yield: about 6 cups.

Opened at Knox and Travis, Dallas, in 1913, Highland Park Pharmacy is still a popular institution.

The Highland Park Pharmacy in the 1940s.

HIGHLAND PARK CHICKEN SALAD SANDWICHES

2 cups chopped cooked
   chicken
¼ cup mayonnaise
1 hard-cooked egg, chopped
3 tablespoons chopped celery
¼ teaspoon salt
⅛ teaspoon white pepper
12 slices whole wheat or
   white bread
Butter or margarine, softened
Pimiento-stuffed or ripe olives
   (optional)

Combine chopped chicken, mayonnaise, egg, celery, salt, and pepper; mix well. Spread ⅓ cup chicken salad evenly on one side of 6 slices of bread. Place the remaining 6 bread slices over the chicken salad to make a sandwich.

Spread butter on outside of top slice of bread; invert sandwiches onto a hot skillet or griddle. Cook until bread is browned. Spread butter on ungrilled side of bread; carefully turn sandwiches, and cook until bread is browned.

Secure sandwiches with wooden picks; cut crosswise into 2 pieces. Serve hot. Garnish with whole olives, if desired. Yield: 6 sandwiches.

SNOWBALLS

Vanilla ice cream
1 cup chopped pecans
1 cup grated coconut
Fudge sauce (recipe follows)

Scoop ice cream into 6 individual balls; refreeze. Roll 3 ice cream balls in chopped pecans,

covering ice cream completely. Roll remaining ice cream balls in coconut, covering ice cream completely. Spoon fudge sauce over ice cream balls, and serve immediately. Yield: 6 servings.

Fudge Sauce:

2 (1-ounce) squares
   unsweetened chocolate
3 tablespoons water
½ cup sugar
Dash of salt
¼ cup plus 2 tablespoons
   butter or margarine,
   softened
½ teaspoon vanilla extract

Combine chocolate and water in top of a double-boiler; cook over boiling water until chocolate melts. Add sugar and salt; cook an additional 5 minutes. Stir in butter and vanilla. Yield: about 1 cup.

LUNCHEON SPECIALITIES

CHICKEN MOUSSE

1 envelope unflavored gelatin
1½ cups cold water, divided
2 teaspoons chicken-flavored
  bouillon granules
¼ teaspoon salt
¼ teaspoon red pepper
½ teaspoon Worcestershire
  sauce
2 teaspoons minced onion
1½ cups diced cooked
  chicken
¼ cup coarsely chopped
  celery
1 tablespoon coarsely
  chopped ripe olives
1 tablespoon chopped
  pimiento
1 tablespoon chopped fresh
  parsley
1 cup whipping cream,
  whipped
Paprika (optional)

Soften gelatin in ½ cup water in a small saucepan. Cook over low heat, stirring constantly, until smooth and thickened. Add bouillon granules, salt, pepper, and Worcestershire sauce, stirring until granules are dissolved. Remove from heat; add remaining water and onion, stirring well. Chill until the consistency of unbeaten egg whites. Gently stir in chicken, celery, olives, pimiento, and parsley. Fold in whipped cream; spoon into a lightly oiled 4-cup mold. Cover, and chill overnight. Sprinkle with paprika, if desired. Serve with crackers. Yield: 4 cups.

A delicate Chicken Mousse.

CURRIED CHICKEN SALAD

2 cups chopped cooked
  chicken
½ cup chopped celery
½ cup slivered almonds,
  toasted
¼ cup sliced water
  chestnuts
½ pound seedless green
  grapes, halved
1 (8-ounce) can pineapple
  tidbits, drained
¾ cup mayonnaise
2 teaspoons lemon juice
2 teaspoons soy sauce
1 teaspoon curry powder
Lettuce leaves

Combine chicken and next 5 ingredients in a medium mixing bowl; mix well. Combine mayonnaise, lemon juice, soy sauce, and curry powder, stirring well; add to chicken mixture. Toss lightly to coat well, and chill.

Serve salad on lettuce leaves. Yield: 6 servings.

There must be as many ways to make Southern chicken salad as there are Southern cooks. We can have it cold or hot, with or without grapes, almonds, or curry. Or we can choose whether to put it into pastry shells. While many people prefer their chicken salad to be made only of white meat, others think the flavor of the dark meat is a valuable addition. One way around this dilemma is to grind the dark meat and cut the white into cubes. Not to play tricks, mind you, but to add the depth of the dark meat's taste to the dish without its intruding itself.

A great many cooks, in making white meat chicken salad, simply substitute turkey breast. This works well enough too, when care is taken to cool the turkey in the broth to ensure that the meat will be moist. Cooks have built reputations on their chicken salad; in Southern small towns one has only to ask whose chicken salad is fairest of them all. The answer will be forthcoming.

To "give a luncheon" today somehow has an old-fashioned connotation. It implies the leisure to prepare it. And, on the part of the guests, the leisure to enjoy it. To many of today's Southern women, busy in the marketplace, the idea of giving a luncheon can evoke responses from downright hilarity to a wistful "Oh, that would be nice, but . . . ."

Luncheons can still be fun, though. They're good for weekends, and men can enjoy them as well.

MARYLAND CHICKEN SALAD

2 cups chopped cooked chicken
1½ cups chopped celery
¾ cup mayonnaise
1 teaspoon salt
¼ teaspoon red pepper
Lettuce leaves
2 hard-cooked eggs, sliced (optional)
1 teaspoon capers (optional)

Combine chicken with next 4 ingredients in a medium mixing bowl; mix well. Chill at least 2 hours.

Serve chicken salad in a lettuce-lined bowl; garnish with egg slices and capers, if desired. Yield: 4 to 6 servings.

CHICKEN SALAD AMANDINE

2 tablespoons mayonnaise
1 tablespoon commercial sour cream
1 tablespoon lemon juice
½ teaspoon salt
⅛ teaspoon white pepper
⅛ teaspoon curry powder
2½ cups chopped cooked chicken
Lettuce leaves
¼ cup slivered almonds, toasted

Combine first 6 ingredients, stirring well; add chicken, and toss lightly to coat well. Chill.

Serve salad on lettuce leaves. Sprinkle with toasted almonds. Yield: 4 servings.

Collection of Bonnie Slotnick

An alfresco luncheon

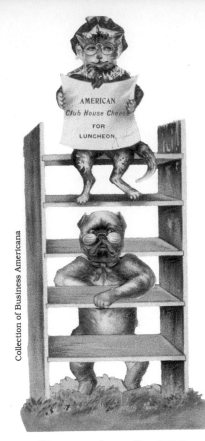

"Buy our cheese!" c.1900.

BAKED CHICKEN SALAD

1 cup chopped cooked
  chicken
½ cup finely chopped celery
¼ cup chopped walnuts
⅓ cup mayonnaise
2 teaspoons lemon juice
1 teaspoon finely chopped
  onion
¼ teaspoon salt
Dash of pepper
½ cup buttered soft
  breadcrumbs or crushed
  potato chips
¼ cup (1 ounce) shredded
  Cheddar cheese

Combine first 8 ingredients; toss gently. Spoon into two 10-ounce buttered custard cups. Top with breadcrumbs or crushed chips. Bake at 400° for 10 minutes. Sprinkle 2 tablespoons cheese on top of each salad; bake an additional 6 minutes. Yield: 2 servings.

CHICKEN SALAD PIES

4 cups chopped cooked
  chicken
1 cup chopped celery
½ cup chopped pecans
¼ cup finely chopped onion
2 hard-cooked eggs, chopped
2 tablespoons lemon juice
½ teaspoon salt
1 cup mayonnaise
Cheese Pastry Shells
2 hard-cooked eggs,
  quartered
Watercress

Combine chicken, celery, pecans, onion, and chopped eggs; toss gently. Stir in lemon juice and salt. Cover and chill. When ready to serve, stir in mayonnaise. Spoon evenly into Cheese Pastry Shells. Garnish with egg quarters and watercress. Yield: 10 servings.

Cheese Pastry Shells:

2 cups all-purpose flour
1 teaspoon salt
⅔ cup shortening
½ cup (2 ounces) shredded
  process American or
  Cheddar cheese
¼ cup cold water

Combine flour and salt; cut in shortening with a pastry blender until mixture resembles coarse meal. Stir in cheese. Sprinkle cold water evenly over surface, stirring with a fork until all dry ingredients are moistened.

Shape dough into 10 balls. Roll to ¼-inch thickness, and fit into ten 3-inch tart pans. Bake at 425° for 10 minutes or until golden brown. Gently remove pastry shells from pans; set aside to cool before filling. Yield: 10 pastry shells.

CHICKEN SALAD IN PATTY SHELLS

3 cups chopped cooked
  chicken
2 cups chopped celery
8 hard-cooked eggs, chopped
½ cup vinegar
1 teaspoon salt
½ teaspoon pepper
1 cup butter or margarine,
  softened
½ cup mayonnaise
12 baked patty shells

Combine first 6 ingredients; toss gently, and set aside.

Combine butter and mayonnaise, beating with a wire whisk until smooth. Pour over chicken mixture; stir well. Spoon into patty shells. Yield: 12 servings.

HOT CHICKEN SANDWICHES

4 slices bread, toasted
4 slices cooked chicken
Cheese Sauce
8 slices bacon, cooked crisp
¼ cup grated Parmesan
  cheese, divided

Place toasted bread on an ovenproof platter. Top each slice of toast with a slice of chicken, ¼ cup Cheese Sauce, 2 slices of bacon, and 1 tablespoon Parmesan cheese. Broil until cheese melts. Yield: 4 sandwiches.

Cheese Sauce:

2 tablespoons butter or
  margarine
2 tablespoons all-purpose
  flour
1 cup milk
1 teaspoon salt
⅛ teaspoon pepper
½ cup (2 ounces) shredded
  process American cheese

Melt butter in a heavy saucepan over low heat; add flour, stirring until smooth. Cook 1 minute, stirring constantly. Gradually add milk; cook over medium heat, stirring constantly, until thickened and bubbly. Add salt, pepper, and cheese; stir until cheese melts. Yield: 1 cup.

Courtesy of Neiman-Marcus

Neiman-Marcus, 1940, the birthplace of the Duke of Windsor Sandwich.

LOUISVILLE HOT BROWN SANDWICHES

Creamy Cheese Sauce
2 egg yolks, beaten
½ cup grated Parmesan
   cheese
1 tablespoon butter or
   margarine
¼ cup whipping cream,
   whipped
4 slices toast
8 ounces cooked chicken,
   thinly sliced
8 slices bacon, cooked

1 cup milk
⅛ teaspoon pepper
¼ cup (1 ounce) shredded
   Cheddar cheese

Melt butter in a heavy saucepan over low heat; add flour, stirring until smooth. Cook 1 minute, stirring constantly. Gradually add milk; cook over medium heat, stirring constantly, until thickened and bubbly. Remove from heat. Add pepper and cheese; stir until cheese melts. Yield: 1 cup.

Combine Creamy Cheese Sauce, yolks, cheese, and butter in top of double boiler; place over boiling water. Reduce heat to low, stirring constantly until cheese and butter are melted. Remove from heat; let cool. Fold in whipped cream.

Trim crust from toast. Arrange toast slices on a lightly greased baking sheet; top each with 2 ounces chicken and ⅓ cup cream sauce. Broil 4 inches from heat until sauce is bubbly. Garnish with bacon slices. Yield: 4 servings.

Creamy Cheese Sauce:

2 tablespoons butter or
   margarine
2 tablespoons all-purpose
   flour

THE DUKE OF WINDSOR SANDWICH

2 pineapple slices
1 tablespoon butter or
   margarine
2½ ounces sharp Cheddar
   cheese spread
6 slices bread, toasted
2 tablespoons chutney
4 slices cooked turkey or
   chicken
Lettuce leaves

Sauté pineapple slices in butter over low heat 5 minutes. Remove from pan; drain and set aside.

Spread cheese on 2 slices of toast. Top each with 1 tablespoon of chutney, 1 slice of toast, 1 sautéed pineapple slice, 2 slices of turkey or chicken, and lettuce leaves. Cover each sandwich with remaining slices of toast. Secure sandwiches with toothpicks; cut into triangles to serve. Yield: 2 servings.

Collection of Bonnie Slotnick

DISHES AND DELICACIES

Chicken Hash: Great hash is no accident and can rise to any occasion.

CHICKEN HASH

4 cups chopped cooked
   chicken
½ cup half-and-half
¼ cup plus 2 tablespoons
   butter or margarine
¼ cup all-purpose flour
1 cup milk
3 egg yolks, lightly beaten
½ teaspoon salt
⅛ teaspoon white pepper
1 cup sliced fresh
   mushrooms
1 teaspoon finely chopped
   onion
½ cup (2 ounces) shredded
   process Swiss cheese,
   divided

Combine chicken and half-and-half in a Dutch oven; cook over low heat 10 minutes, and set aside.

Melt butter in a heavy sauce-pan over low heat; add flour, and stir until smooth. Cook 1 minute, stirring constantly. Gradually add milk; cook over medium heat, stirring constantly, until thickened and bubbly.

Stir ¼ cup of the hot white sauce into egg yolks; add to remaining hot sauce mixture, stirring constantly. Stir in salt and pepper.

Add half of sauce to chicken mixture in Dutch oven; stir well. Pour chicken mixture into a well-greased 2-quart casserole. Sprinkle mushrooms evenly over chicken mixture. Add onion and ¼ cup cheese to the remaining sauce; stir well, and pour over mushrooms. Sprinkle with remaining cheese. Broil 6 inches from heat for 7 minutes or until top is lightly browned. Yield: 8 servings.

TURKEY HASH

1 tablespoon finely chopped
   onion
3 tablespoons butter or
   margarine
1 cup well-seasoned
   gravy
¼ cup whipping cream
1 teaspoon celery salt
⅛ teaspoon pepper
3 cups chopped cooked
   turkey
Cornbread squares (optional)

Sauté onion in butter in a large saucepan until tender. Stir in remaining ingredients. Cook over medium heat, stirring constantly, 3 minutes or until thoroughly heated. Spoon hash over cornbread, if desired. Yield: 4 servings.

Note: For well-seasoned gravy, use any prepared gravy mix or Roast Fowl Gravy (page 49).

"A wonderful lift for breakfast on blue Monday," opens the old Virginia recipe for Chicken Omelet. "Make extra gravy with the Sunday chicken and pick all the chicken bones, using a knife to cut up into small pieces, skin, meat, wing tip, etc...." it continues, until the reader is simply starving for that omelet. Further, it is another reminder of the utter frugality of the cook. She had probably raised that bird from the egg, killed and dressed it, and gathered the wood for the fire that cooked it; not a morsel was wasted. Old recipes do carry many hidden messages.

Another jog is supplied to the memory when we refer to the original recipe for Chicken in a Shell. The early housekeeper was woefully short of kitchen utensils, and the scallop shell was to her a practical dish for baking individual servings. The shells were also used as sauce dishes.

There are many lovely entrees in this chapter: satisfying hashes and scallops, chicken combined with the South's other favorite food, cornbread, for a beautiful shortcake, or turkey combined with sausage for a special dinner that's as tempting to look at as it is to eat—whole cranberry sauce is ladled over each serving.

These dishes can be luncheons, dinners, or suppers, useful in almost any context. Most importantly, they're good!

Sane advice for the poultry farmer in this ad, c.1900.

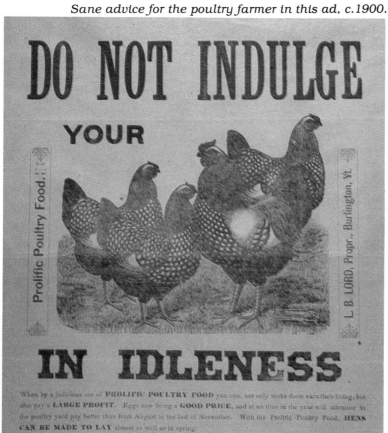

Collection of Business Americana

GEORGIA CHICKEN SCALLOP

⅓ cup uncooked regular rice
2 cups chicken broth
2½ cups diced cooked chicken
2 eggs, beaten
⅓ cup chopped celery
¼ cup chopped pimiento
¾ teaspoon salt
⅛ teaspoon poultry seasoning
Mushroom sauce (recipe follows)

Combine rice and broth in a medium saucepan; bring to a boil. Cover; reduce heat, and simmer 10 minutes.

Add chicken, eggs, celery, pimiento, salt, and poultry seasoning to rice mixture; stir well. Spoon into a well-greased 10- x 6- x 2-inch baking dish. Bake at 325° for 1 hour and 5 minutes. Serve hot with mushroom sauce. Yield: 6 servings.

Mushroom Sauce:

½ medium onion, minced
3 tablespoons butter or margarine
3 tablespoons flour
1 cup chicken broth
½ cup whipping cream
1 (6-ounce) jar sliced mushrooms, drained
¼ teaspoon salt
Dash of pepper

Sauté onion in butter in a small saucepan over low heat until tender. Add flour, stirring until smooth. Cook 1 minute, stirring constantly. Gradually add broth and whipping cream; cook over medium heat, stirring constantly, until thickened and bubbly. Stir in remaining ingredients. Yield: 2¼ cups.

CHICKEN IN A SHELL

4 cups chopped cooked
  chicken
½ cup sherry
¼ cup butter or margarine,
  divided
2 tablespoons all-purpose
  flour
1½ cups half-and-half
½ pound fresh mushrooms,
  sliced
2 tablespoons chopped fresh
  parsley
1 teaspoon salt
Dash of red pepper
3 tablespoons fine, dry
  breadcrumbs

Soak chicken in sherry 1
hour; drain well, and set aside.
Discard sherry.

Melt 2 tablespoons butter in a
large saucepan over low heat;
add flour, stirring until smooth.
Cook 1 minute, stirring constantly. Gradually add half-and-
half; cook over medium heat,
stirring constantly, until thickened and bubbly. Remove from
heat. Add reserved chicken, and
stir well.

Sauté mushrooms in remaining butter in a small skillet 3 to
5 minutes. Add mushrooms,
parsley, salt, and pepper to
chicken mixture; stir well. Divide chicken mixture among 8
scallop shells or ramekins. Top
with breadcrumbs. Bake at 375°
for 25 minutes or until lightly
browned. Yield: 8 servings.

*Chicken in a Shell (left),
easy to make if the cook
has a modern contraption
like the one above to make
the breadcrumb topping.*

PLANTATION
CHICKEN CASSEROLE

¼ cup cornmeal
1 teaspoon salt
1 cup boiling water
2 eggs, beaten
1 cup milk
1 teaspoon baking powder
2 tablespoons butter or
  margarine, melted
2 cups chopped cooked
  chicken

Combine cornmeal and salt;
add water, stirring constantly
until well blended; cool.

Combine eggs and milk; add
to cornmeal mixture, stirring
gently until smooth. Stir in baking powder, butter, and
chicken. Pour into a well-
greased 1-quart casserole; bake
at 375° for 40 to 45 minutes.
Yield: 4 servings.

Note: Two cups chopped
cooked turkey may be substituted for chicken.

TURKEY AU GRATIN

2 tablespoons butter or
  margarine
½ cup chopped celery
2 tablespoons all-purpose
  flour
1½ cups milk
1½ cups chopped cooked
  turkey
½ teaspoon salt
⅛ teaspoon pepper
¼ cup buttered soft
  breadcrumbs

Melt butter in a heavy saucepan over low heat; add celery,
and cook 5 minutes or until
tender. Add flour, stirring until
smooth. Cook 1 minute, stirring constantly. Gradually add
milk; cook over medium heat,
stirring constantly, until thickened and bubbly. Add turkey,
salt, and pepper to white sauce,
stirring well.

Spoon mixture into a lightly
greased 1-quart casserole; top
with breadcrumbs. Bake at 400°
for 30 minutes or until breadcrumbs are browned. Yield: 4
servings.

A fine-feathered friend

TURKEY-SAUSAGE
CASSEROLE

½ pound mild bulk pork
  sausage
¼ cup butter or margarine
¼ cup all-purpose flour
2½ cups milk
¼ teaspoon paprika
¼ teaspoon salt
⅛ teaspoon pepper
3 cups cubed cooked turkey
½ cup soft breadcrumbs
1 teaspoon butter or
  margarine
Cranberry sauce (optional)

Brown sausage in a small skillet, stirring to crumble; drain
well, and set aside.

Melt ¼ cup butter in a large
saucepan over low heat; add
flour, stirring until smooth.
Cook 1 minute, stirring constantly. Gradually add milk;
cook over medium heat, stirring
constantly, until thickened and
bubbly. Add paprika, salt, pepper, and turkey, stirring well.

Spoon half the turkey mixture
into a well-greased 1½-quart
casserole. Sprinkle half the sausage over turkey. Repeat layers;
sprinkle top with breadcrumbs,
and dot with 1 teaspoon butter.
Bake, uncovered, at 400° for 30
minutes. Serve with cranberry
sauce, if desired. Yield: 4 to 6
servings.

TURKEY SOUFFLÉ

4½ tablespoons butter or margarine
¼ cup plus 2 tablespoons all-purpose flour
1½ cups milk
½ teaspoon salt
1 cup finely chopped cooked turkey
3 eggs, separated

Melt butter in a heavy saucepan over low heat; add flour, stirring until smooth. Cook 1 minute, stirring constantly. Gradually add milk; cook over medium heat, stirring constantly, until thickened and bubbly. Remove from heat; stir in salt and turkey.

Beat egg yolks in a small mixing bowl until thick and lemon colored; gradually stir in one-fourth of hot turkey mixture. Combine yolk mixture with remaining hot mixture, stirring constantly.

Beat egg whites (at room temperature) until stiff but not dry; gently fold into turkey mixture. Spoon into a lightly greased 1½-quart soufflé dish. Bake at 325° for 1 hour or until golden brown. Yield: 6 servings.

Note: 1 cup finely chopped cooked chicken may be substituted for turkey.

Turkey Spoonbread to be savored with a luscious giblet gravy.

TURKEY SPOONBREAD

5 cups turkey or chicken broth
1 cup white cornmeal
2 tablespoons tapioca
2 teaspoons salt
⅓ cup butter or margarine, softened
5 eggs, separated
4 cups chopped cooked turkey
Giblet gravy (recipe follows)

Combine first 4 ingredients in the top of a double boiler. Place over boiling water; cook 1 minute or until thickened, stirring constantly. Add butter; stir until butter is melted. Cool slightly.

Beat egg yolks until thick and lemon colored. Stir egg yolks and turkey into cornmeal mixture. Beat egg whites (at room temperature) until stiff but not dry; gently fold into cornmeal mixture. Pour into a lightly greased shallow 2-quart baking dish. Bake at 350° for 1 hour or until a knife inserted in center comes out clean. Serve giblet gravy over spoonbread. Yield: 8 to 10 servings.

Giblet Gravy:

3 tablespoons shortening
3 tablespoons all-purpose flour
2 cups turkey or chicken broth
¼ cup chopped cooked giblets
1 hard-cooked egg, chopped
¼ teaspoon salt
⅛ teaspoon pepper

Melt shortening in a large skillet over low heat. Add flour, stirring until smooth. Cook 1 minute, stirring constantly. Gradually add broth; cook over medium heat, stirring constantly, until thickened and bubbly. Stir in remaining ingredients. Yield: 2 cups.

Right: "A Wild Turkey Hunt, July 5th," *from Lewis Miller's sketchbook.*

A wild Turkey Hunt, July 5.th

Mr Elizah Ingles and his little Brothers
coming home, he Shot two an old and young one
A large fine turkey.

CHICKEN OMELET

1 cup chopped cooked
chicken
¾ cup well-seasoned chicken
gravy
6 eggs, separated
¼ cup plus 2 tablespoons
milk
Salt and pepper to taste
1 tablespoon butter or
margarine
Fresh parsley sprigs (optional)

Combine chicken and gravy
in a small saucepan; heat
thoroughly.

Beat egg yolks until thick and
lemon colored. Stir in milk, salt,
and pepper. Beat egg whites (at
room temperature) until stiff
peaks form; gently fold into yolk
mixture.

Melt butter in a large ovenproof skillet over medium heat.
Remove from heat. Pour egg
mixture into hot skillet. Bake at
350° for 20 minutes or until
knife inserted 1 inch from edge
of skillet comes out clean.

Slide omelet onto a large
warm serving platter. Spoon
half of chicken mixture over
omelet; fold omelet in half, and
spoon remaining chicken mixture around sides. Garnish with
parsley sprigs, if desired. Serve
the omelet immediately. Yield: 4
to 6 servings.

Note: For well-seasoned gravy,
use any prepared gravy mix or
Roast Fowl Gravy (page 49).

VIRGINIA CREAMED CHICKEN

¼ cup butter or margarine
¼ cup all-purpose flour
1½ cups milk
½ teaspoon salt
Dash of red pepper
1 cup diced cooked chicken
1 tablespoon sherry
6 slices toast

Melt butter in a heavy saucepan over low heat; add flour,
stirring until smooth. Cook 1
minute, stirring constantly.
Gradually add milk; cook over
medium heat, stirring constantly, until thickened and
bubbly. Stir in salt and pepper.
Add chicken; cook until chicken
is thoroughly heated. Stir in
sherry. Spoon over toast slices.
Yield: 6 servings.

CHICKEN À LA KING

1 hard-cooked egg
3½ tablespoons butter or
margarine, divided
¼ pound fresh mushrooms,
sliced
1½ tablespoons chopped
green pepper
2 tablespoons all-purpose
flour
1½ cups milk
2 cups chopped cooked
chicken
½ teaspoon salt
⅛ teaspoon pepper
1½ tablespoons chopped
pimiento
Toast Cups
Fresh parsley sprigs
(optional)

Crumble egg yolk; finely grate
egg white, and set aside.

Melt 1½ tablespoons butter in
a saucepan over low heat. Add
mushrooms and green pepper;
sauté until tender. Set aside.

Melt remaining butter in a
large skillet over low heat; add
flour, and stir until smooth.
Cook 1 minute, stirring constantly. Gradually add milk;
cook over medium heat, stirring
constantly, until thickened and
bubbly.

Add crumbled yolk, chicken,
salt, pepper, pimiento, and sautéed vegetables to white sauce.
Spoon mixture into toast cups;
sprinkle with grated egg white.
Garnish with parsley, if desired.
Yield: 8 servings.

Toast Cups:

8 slices bread
Softened butter or margarine

Trim crust from bread slices;
lightly butter both sides. Press
each slice into a 10-ounce custard cup. Bake at 350° for 15
minutes or until lightly
browned. Yield: 8 toast cups.

Farmer Brand egg label, late 1800

Abby Aldrich Rockefeller Folk Art Center, Williamsburg, Virginia

Rooster, a favorite model for artists for centuries, appears here carved in pine. Middle 1800s.

DIXIE CHICKEN SHORTCAKE

1 cup chicken broth, divided
1 tablespoon all-purpose flour
½ pound fresh mushrooms, sliced
1 tablespoon butter or margarine
2 cups diced cooked chicken
⅛ teaspoon pepper
Salt to taste
Southern Cornbread

Place ½ cup broth in a medium saucepan over low heat; add flour, and stir until smooth. Cook 1 minute, stirring con-

stantly. Gradually add remaining ½ cup broth; cook over medium heat, stirring constantly, until thickened and bubbly. Set aside.

Sauté mushrooms in butter in a small skillet 3 to 5 minutes. Stir mushrooms, chicken, and seasonings into white sauce.

To serve, slice individual cornbread squares in half horizontally; spoon chicken mixture over the bottom half of each square. Replace top half of each square, and spoon about 1 tablespoon of chicken mixture over top. Yield: 9 servings.

Southern Cornbread:

1 cup cornmeal
½ teaspoon baking soda
½ teaspoon salt
1 egg, beaten
1 cup buttermilk
1 tablespoon shortening, melted

Combine dry ingredients; add egg, buttermilk, and shortening, mixing well. Pour batter into a well-greased 8-inch square pan. Bake at 450° for 20 minutes or until lightly browned. Cut cornbread into squares. Yield: 9 servings.

123

RING AROUND CHICKEN

¼ cup butter or margarine
½ cup all-purpose flour
3 cups chicken broth
½ cup milk
3 cups chopped cooked chicken
½ cup sliced ripe olives
2 tablespoons chopped pimiento
1 teaspoon salt
⅛ teaspoon pepper
Biscuit Ring

Melt butter in a large, heavy saucepan over low heat; add flour, stirring until smooth. Cook 1 minute, stirring constantly. Gradually add broth and milk; cook over medium heat, stirring constantly, until thickened and bubbly. Stir in chicken, olives, pimiento, salt, and pepper. Spoon creamed chicken over Biscuit Ring. Serve immediately. Yield: 12 servings.

Biscuit Ring:

4 cups self-rising flour
1 tablespoon baking powder
1 tablespoon sugar
¾ cup shortening
2 cups buttermilk

Combine flour, baking powder, and sugar; stir well. Cut in shortening with a pastry blender until mixture resembles coarse meal. Sprinkle buttermilk evenly over flour mixture, stirring until dry ingredients are moistened.

Spoon dough into a lightly greased 6-cup ovenproof ring mold. Bake at 400° for 15 minutes or until lightly browned. Yield: one 9-inch ring.

CHICKEN CROQUETTES

1 tablespoon butter or margarine
1 tablespoon finely chopped onion
1 tablespoon all-purpose flour
¾ cup chicken broth
½ teaspoon dry mustard
½ teaspoon salt
Dash red pepper
4 cups finely chopped cooked chicken
2 egg yolks, beaten
¼ cup sherry
1 cup cracker crumbs
Vegetable oil

Melt butter in a large, heavy saucepan over low heat; add onion, and cook until tender. Add flour, stirring until smooth. Cook 1 minute, stirring constantly. Gradually add broth; cook over medium heat, stirring constantly, until thickened and bubbly. Stir in mustard, salt, pepper, and chicken. Add egg yolks. Cook over medium heat, stirring constantly, 3 to 5 minutes. Remove from heat, and chill mixture thoroughly. Stir in sherry.

Shape mixture into croquettes, and roll in cracker crumbs. Deep fry croquettes in hot oil (375°) until golden brown. Drain on paper towels. Yield: 14 croquettes.

Chicken Croquettes: Some tearooms once specialized in them.

A Texas farm family poses among tall cornstalks.

CHICKEN FIESTA

½ cup butter or margarine
½ cup all-purpose flour
4 cups chicken broth
6 cups chopped cooked
   chicken
½ teaspoon salt
¼ teaspoon pepper
Fiesta Cornbread

Melt butter in a heavy sauce-pan over low heat; add flour, stirring until smooth. Cook 1 minute, stirring constantly. Gradually add broth; cook over medium heat, stirring constantly, until thickened and bubbly. Stir in chicken, salt, and pepper. Spoon creamed chicken over Fiesta Cornbread squares. Serve immediately. Yield: 12 servings.

Fiesta Cornbread:

1 cup cornmeal
1 teaspoon salt
1 (17-ounce) can cream-style
   corn
1 (14½-ounce) can whole
   tomatoes, undrained
1 cup (4 ounces) shredded
   sharp Cheddar cheese
1 cup milk
2 medium onions, chopped
2 eggs
1 (4-ounce) can chopped
   green chiles, drained

Combine cornmeal and salt; mix well. Stir in remaining in-gredients. Pour batter into a lightly greased 13- x 9- x 2-inch baking pan. Bake at 350° for 1 hour and 20 minutes or until a wooden pick inserted in center comes out clean. Cool 10 min-utes in pan. Cut into squares to serve. Yield: 12 servings.

CREAMED TURKEY IN SHELLS

6 whole English muffins
1 cup diced cooked turkey
1 cup well-seasoned, thick
   gravy
2 tablespoons chopped onion
2 tablespoons chopped fresh
   parsley
Fresh parsley sprigs (optional)

Split muffins; scoop out cen-ter, leaving a ½-inch shell. Place muffin shells on a baking sheet, and bake at 350° for 8 minutes or until lightly browned.

Combine turkey, gravy, onion, and parsley in a medium saucepan; cook over medium heat 15 minutes. Spoon turkey mixture into muffin shells; gar-nish with parsley, if desired. Yield: 6 servings.

Note: For well-seasoned gravy, use any prepared gravy mix or Roast Fowl Gravy (page 49).

WASTE NOT . . .

CHICKEN LIVER APPETIZERS

½ cup all-purpose flour
½ teaspoon salt
¼ teaspoon pepper
1 pound chicken livers, cut
  into bite-size pieces
Sweet and Sour Plum Sauce

Combine first 3 ingredients; mix well. Dredge livers in flour mixture.

Fry livers, a few at a time, in deep hot oil (350°) for 3 minutes or until golden brown. Drain livers well on paper towels. Serve immediately with Sweet and Sour Plum Sauce. Yield: about 2 dozen.

Sweet and Sour Plum Sauce:

¾ cup plum jam
3 tablespoons chutney
1½ teaspoons vinegar
⅛ teaspoon hot sauce

Combine all ingredients in a small saucepan; cook until thoroughly heated. Serve hot or cold. Store in refrigerator. Yield: about ¾ cup.

CHICKEN LIVER PÂTÉ

1 cup butter or margarine,
  divided
2 pounds chicken livers
2 medium onions, chopped
1 small cooking apple, peeled,
  cored, and grated
2 teaspoons curry powder
¾ teaspoon salt
¼ teaspoon pepper
2 tablespoons brandy
2 hard-cooked eggs (optional)
Fresh parsley sprigs (optional)

Melt ½ cup butter in a large skillet. Add livers, onion, apple, curry powder, salt, and pepper. Cook over medium-low heat, stirring occasionally, 30 minutes or until liquid is absorbed.

Spoon liver mixture into container of blender or food processor; process until smooth. Cut remaining butter into 4 pieces.

Chicken Liver Pâté: No cocktail party should be without it.

Add butter and brandy; process until smooth.

Spoon mixture into a lightly oiled 3½-cup mold. Chill several hours or overnight. Invert onto serving platter; garnish with chopped or sliced hard-cooked eggs and parsley, if desired. Serve pâté with crackers. Yield: 3½ cups.

CHICKEN LIVERS IN WINE

6 slices bacon
½ cup all-purpose flour
½ teaspoon salt
⅛ teaspoon pepper
1 pound chicken livers
½ cup dry white wine
2 teaspoons chopped fresh
  parsley
Hot cooked rice or toast
  points

Cook bacon in a large skillet until crisp; drain on paper towels. Crumble and set aside, reserving ¼ cup drippings in skillet.

Combine flour, salt, and pepper in a plastic or paper bag; shake to mix. Place 3 or 4 livers in bag; shake well. Repeat procedure with remaining livers. Brown livers in reserved bacon drippings. Reduce heat, and stir in wine. Cover, and simmer 5 minutes or until livers are done. Sprinkle reserved bacon and parsley over livers. Serve over rice or toast points. Yield: 6 servings.

First-prize winner of the America Cup, a Brown Leghorn cock.

SPAGHETTI CARUSO

1 large onion, chopped
1 small green pepper,
  chopped
2 cloves garlic, minced
¼ cup plus 2 tablespoons
  olive oil, divided
1 (28-ounce) can pear-shaped
  tomatoes, undrained and
  chopped
1 (15-ounce) can tomato
  sauce
1 teaspoon dried whole basil
½ teaspoon ground oregano
½ teaspoon salt
¼ teaspoon pepper
1 pound chicken livers,
  quartered
1 (12-ounce) package thin
  spaghetti
Grated Parmesan cheese
  (optional)

Sauté onion, green pepper, and garlic in a large, heavy, ovenproof skillet in ¼ cup olive oil until vegetables are tender. Add tomatoes, tomato sauce, basil, oregano, salt, and pepper, stirring well. Cover and bake at 350° for 1 hour and 30 minutes, stirring occasionally.

Sauté chicken livers in remaining olive oil for five minutes. Combine chicken livers and sauce, stirring well. Cover and simmer an additional 10 minutes.

Prepare spaghetti according to package directions. Serve sauce over spaghetti. Sprinkle with Parmesan cheese, if desired. Yield: 6 to 8 servings.

In making Chicken Liver Pâté, it is good to know that lining the oiled mold with plastic wrap before adding the liver mixture will help greatly at unmolding time. Just make sure the plastic ends are all outside the mold. Place the serving dish over it, invert, and tug on the plastic wrap. The mold will drop right out, and the plastic comes off cleanly.

A thought on cooking chicken livers: if they are not to be cut into pieces before frying, they should be pricked a couple of times with a skewer to prevent their popping and spattering hot fat on the surrounding areas, including the cook.

Henry Morrison Flagler and family at the Hotel Ponce de Leon, St. Augustine, Florida. c.1905.

CHICKEN LIVERS FINANCIÈRE

½ pound fresh mushrooms, sliced
½ cup minced green onion
½ cup plus 2 tablespoons butter or margarine, divided
¾ cup beef broth
Brown sauce (recipe follows)
16 pimiento-stuffed olives, sliced
¼ cup lemon juice
⅛ teaspoon red pepper
2 pounds chicken livers
½ teaspoon salt
¼ cup cognac
Hot cooked rice

Sauté mushrooms and onion in 2 tablespoons butter in a large skillet until tender. Add broth, 1½ cups brown sauce, olives, lemon juice, and pepper, stirring well. Cook over medium heat 5 minutes, stirring constantly. Remove from heat, and set aside.

Wash livers; pat dry, and sprinkle with salt. Sauté livers in remaining butter in a large skillet 5 minutes or until livers are lightly browned. Warm cognac; ignite and pour over livers in skillet. Transfer livers to serving platter with hot cooked rice, reserving pan drippings in skillet. Add reserved mushroom mixture to pan drippings, stirring well; heat thoroughly. Spoon mixture over livers; serve immediately. Yield: 8 servings.

Brown Sauce:

¾ cup coarsely chopped onion
¾ cup coarsely chopped carrots
¼ cup plus 2 tablespoons butter or margarine
¼ cup plus 2 tablespoons all-purpose flour
3½ cups beef broth
1½ cups Chablis or other dry white wine
2 stalks celery, chopped
3 sprigs fresh parsley
1 small bay leaf
2 cloves garlic
½ teaspoon ground thyme
¼ teaspoon coarsely ground black pepper
1 tablespoon tomato paste

Sauté onion and carrots in butter in a large Dutch oven for 10 minutes. Add flour, stirring constantly, until flour is browned. Stir in next 8 ingredients; simmer, uncovered, stirring occasionally, 1 hour or until sauce is reduced by half. Stir in tomato paste. Remove from heat, and strain sauce, discarding vegetables. Refrigerate remaining sauce for other uses. Yield: about 2½ cups.

CHICKEN LIVER OMELET

⅓ cup all-purpose flour
¾ teaspoon salt, divided
¼ teaspoon pepper, divided
¾ cup chicken livers, diced
¼ cup butter or margarine,
  divided
3 eggs
3 tablespoons water

Combine flour, ¼ teaspoon salt, and ⅛ teaspoon pepper; mix well. Dredge livers in flour mixture; brown in 3 tablespoons butter. Cook over medium heat 5 minutes or until livers are done.

Combine eggs, water, and remaining salt and pepper; beat well. Heat a 10-inch omelet pan or skillet until hot enough to sizzle a drop of water. Add remaining 1 tablespoon butter; rotate pan to coat bottom.

Pour egg mixture quickly into pan. Shake pan vigorously (or use spatula to lift cooked portion) so that uncooked portion flows underneath. Slide pan back and forth over heat to keep mixture in motion.

Spoon livers over half of omelet when eggs are set and top is still moist and creamy. Fold unfilled side over filling. Serve omelet immediately. Yield: 2 servings.

DIRTY RICE

1 pound chicken livers
1 cup chopped onion, divided
1 clove garlic
½ teaspoon salt
½ cup chopped green pepper
½ cup chopped celery
2 tablespoons butter or
  margarine
½ teaspoon ground thyme
6 cups cooked rice

Combine livers, ½ cup onion, garlic, salt, and water to cover in a medium saucepan; bring to a boil. Cover; reduce heat, and simmer 20 minutes or until livers are tender. Strain broth, reserving livers. Pat livers dry; process in food processor or put through a food mill until coarsely ground. Sauté remaining onion, green pepper, and celery in butter in a large skillet. Stir in thyme, ground livers, and rice. Gently spoon mixture into a greased 2-quart baking dish; bake, uncovered, at 350° for 30 minutes or until lightly browned. Yield: 6 to 8 servings.

TURKEY BONE SOUP

1 turkey carcass
6 quarts water
3 stalks celery
1 medium onion, quartered
¼ cup chopped turkey giblets
¼ cup chopped fresh parsley
1 teaspoon salt
½ teaspoon pepper

Combine all ingredients in a large Dutch oven. Bring to a boil; cover and simmer 2 hours. Strain soup, and discard carcass and vegetables. Yield: about 3 quarts.

Note: This recipe results in a rich broth which should be used as the base for other recipes. The carcass and giblets from a baked or roasted chicken, capon, duck, or goose may be prepared in the same way, and substituted for the turkey.

Child on early advertising card shows low resistance to a brand of soup.

Collection of Business Americana

TRADE MARK
REGISTERED

"NONE BETTER
CAN BE MADE"

GOOD TO KNOW

PURCHASING

Check the appropriate labels which indicate that the poultry has been inspected, rated Grade A, and is not older than the expiration date. Select poultry with short legs, plump body, unbruised skin, and a good fatty layer. If packaged, check to see that the package is unbroken.

The amount of chicken to be purchased depends on the number of people to be served.

- Allow one-fourth to one-half chicken per person for broiling or frying.

- Allow ½ pound uncooked chicken per person for roasting or stewing.

The size turkey to be purchased depends on the number of people to be served; 16- to 24-pound turkeys yield more meat per pound than smaller birds.

- For a 5- to 12-pound turkey, allow ¾ to 1 pound uncooked meat per person.

- For a 12- to 24-pound turkey, allow ½ to ¾ pound uncooked meat per person.

POULTRY PURCHASING GUIDE

Variety	Market Form	Average Weight in Pounds	Approximate Amount to Buy per Serving	Cooking Methods
Chicken (whole)	Broiler-fryer	1½ to 3½	½ lb.	bake, broil fry, grill roast, simmer
	Roaster	3½ to 5	½ lb.	bake, roast
	Stewing chicken	4½ to 6	½ lb.	simmer, stew
	Capon	4 to 7	½ lb.	bake, broil fry, roast
	Rock Cornish Hens	1½ or less	1 hen	broil, fry roast
Chicken (parts)	Chicken Pieces	1½ to 3½	2 pieces	bake, fry grill, simmer
	Chicken Halves	1½ to 2½	1 half	bake, broil grill
	Chicken Quarters	2½	1 quarter	bake, broil fry, grill
	Drumsticks		2 pieces	fry, grill
	Thighs		2 pieces	fry, grill
	Breasts	1½ to 2	½ breast	bake, broil fry, grill
	Wings		2 wings	fry, grill
	Chicken Livers		¼ pound	broil, fry simmer
Turkey	Fryer-Roaster	4 to 9	For a bird 11 lbs. or less, ¾ to 1 lb.	bake, grill roast
	Young Hen	8 to 14		bake, grill roast
	Young Tom	12 and up	For a bird 12 lbs. or more, ½ to ¾ lb.	bake, grill roast
Duck	Duckling	4 to 6	1 lb.	bake, roast
Goose	Young Goose	6 to 12	1 lb.	bake, roast
Squab	Squab	¾-1¼	2 squab	bake, roast

REFRIGERATING

Fresh poultry and products labeled "Keep under refrigeration" should be purchased only if they have been under refrigeration in the store.

Refrigerate poultry as soon as possible after purchase. When refrigerating, remove all store wrappings, and wash thoroughly in cold running water. Remove the giblets and liver, and wash. Wrap the poultry, giblets, and liver loosely in plastic wrap or foil.

- Fresh whole chicken will keep in the refrigerator for 2 to 3 days.

- Fresh cut-up chicken will keep in the refrigerator for 2 days.

- Fresh whole turkey will keep in the refrigerator for 4 to 5 days.

- Giblets and liver should be cooked within 24 hours.

FREEZING

All poultry should be frozen at zero degrees or less. To prepare for freezing, remove all store wrappings, wash thoroughly in cold running water, pat dry, and wrap tightly in plastic wrap, foil, or freezer paper. Squeeze out as much air as possible from wrapped package.

- Whole chickens can be frozen up to 12 months.

- Cut-up chicken and whole turkeys can be frozen up to 6 months.

THAWING

Frozen poultry should not be allowed to thaw on work surfaces or on refrigerator shelves where other foods are to be placed.

Bargaining for the "perfect" turkey. Durham, North Carolina, 1939.

FRYING

For deep frying, fill utensil no more than one-third full with vegetable or olive oil. Heat oil to medium high temperature or 360°.

To check oil temperature without a thermometer, drop a bread cube or a teaspoonful of batter into the hot oil. If it sizzles instantly and browns, the oil has reached 360°. The meat is done when a fork can be inserted with ease.

Chicken pieces will look larger if dipped in beaten egg and rolled in cracker crumbs before frying.

ROASTING

Variations in ovens, shape of poultry, and degree of thawing will affect roasting time. It is important to begin checking for doneness about 1 hour before the end of the recommended roasting time. Several methods may be used:

- Use a meat thermometer and cook poultry to internal temperature indicated on roasting chart.

- Move leg up and down and pinch meat with fingers protected with paper towels; the leg should move easily at the joint and the meat feel soft when pinched.

- Prick the drumstick with a fork to see that the juices run clear.

STUFFING

When interchanging stuffing recipes, allow ½ cup stuffing per pound of uncooked poultry (i.e., a 6-pound turkey would require 3 cups stuffing).

Always stuff poultry immediately before roasting. If poultry is stuffed and then refrigerated, the center of the chilled stuffing may not reach the proper heat (160°) to destroy the salmonella germ (which causes food poisoning) by the time the meat is done. This is especially true of large turkeys. Stuffing should be lightly packed to allow heat penetration and complete cooking.

STEWING AND SIMMERING

Simmered chicken is excellent for chicken salad, casseroles, pot pies, and creamed chicken dishes. A 3-pound broiler-fryer yields about 2½ cups cut-up chicken and 2 to 2½ cups broth. (*See* page 17 for recipe)

- Chicken broth may be stored safely in the refrigerator for 2 weeks.

POULTRY ROASTING TIMETABLE

Variety (unstuffed)*	Ready-to-Cook Weight in Pounds	Oven Temperature	Approx. Roasting Time in Hours	Final Internal Temperature
Chicken	1½ to 2	400°F	¾ to 1	185°F
	2 to 2½	375°F	1 to 1¼	185°F
	2½ to 3	375°F	1¼ to 1½	185°F
	3 to 4	375°F	1½ to 2	185°F
	4 to 5	375°F	2 to 2½	185°F
Capon	4 to 7	375°F	2½ to 3	185°F
Cornish Hen	1 to 1½	375°F	1¼ to 1½	185°F
Duckling	3 to 5	375°F	1½ to 2	190°F
Goose	7 to 9	350°F	2½ to 3	190°F
	9 to 11	350°F	3 to 3½	190°F
	11 to 13	350°F	3½ to 4	190°F
Turkey	6 to 8	325°F	3 to 3½	185°F
	8 to 12	325°F	3½ to 4	185°F
	12 to 16	325°F	4 to 4½	185°F
	16 to 20	325°F	4½ to 5½	185°F
	20 to 24	325°F	5½ to 6½	185°F

*Add about ½ hour to roasting time for stuffed poultry.

The wrong way to carve

. . .and the right

- The broth may be frozen in ice trays, transferred to plastic bags, and kept frozen for 6 months, ready for handy seasoning.

The broth is excellent as a soup or consommé or as a seasoning for meat and vegetable dishes. It may be substituted for commercial canned broth or bouillon cubes or granules in many recipes.

The strained broth should be placed in the refrigerator to chill while still warm. The chicken fat which accumulates on top may be skimmed off. (It has been said that the flakiest pie crust is made by substituting chicken fat for the lard or shortening in the pastry recipe.)

COOKING DUMPLINGS

When cooking dumplings, it is very important to keep the cooking utensil covered throughout the cooking process in order to take full advantage of the steaming process. (If you must watch, cover the utensil with a glass pie plate.)

The dumplings should be placed in a Dutch oven or other large utensil without crowding to allow room for expansion during cooking.

STORING COOKED POULTRY DISHES

Refrigerate leftover poultry dishes promptly without waiting for the food to reach room temperature. Remove meat from the bones as soon as possible.

- Cooked poultry with or without liquid will keep in the refrigerator up to 2 days.
- Cooked poultry with liquid may be frozen up to 6 months, without liquid up to 1 month.

- Remove the stuffing from the bird and store in a separate container.
- Stuffing and gravy may be refrigerated for 3 to 4 days or frozen up to 2 months.

CARVING PROCEDURES

Allow the bird to stand at least 15 minutes before carving.

Use the proper carving utensils, selecting a knife with a very sharp edge and long flexible blade, and a large two-tined carving fork. Carving may be done from the platter at the table or on a cutting board.

Place the bird, breast side up, on the platter or cutting board and insert the carving fork to steady the bird.

Cut the skin between the thigh and breast, bending the leg away from the body of the bird and exposing the hip joint. Slice through the joint to remove the whole leg.

Locate the joint between the thigh and drumstick, cutting down through the joint to separate the thigh and drumstick. When carving a turkey, slice the dark meat from the bones rather than placing the whole thigh and drumstick on the serving platter.

Remove the wing by cutting diagonally through the breast toward the wing. Move the wing to locate the shoulder joint, and slice through the joint to remove the wing.

To carve the breast, hold the bird securely with the carving fork. Beginning at the meaty area above the shoulder joint, cut thin slices diagonally through the meat (across the grain) the entire length of the breast.

Carve from one side of the bird at a time, carving only as much meat as needed to serve.

DEBONING A CHICKEN BREAST

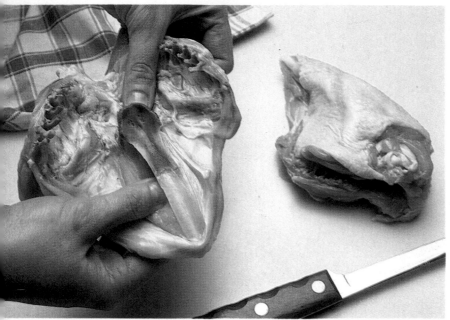

Step 1—Cut the chicken breast in half by removing the keel bone first. Bend back the breast, exposing the keel bone. Loosen the meat from the bone by placing the thumbs under the bone and running around both sides. Pull out bone cartilage.

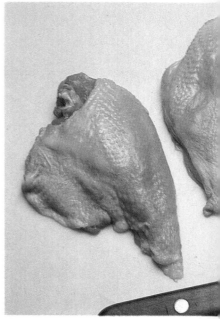

Step 2—With a sharp boning knife or other sharp long bladed knife, cut the chicken breast in half using the outline left by the keel bone as a guide.

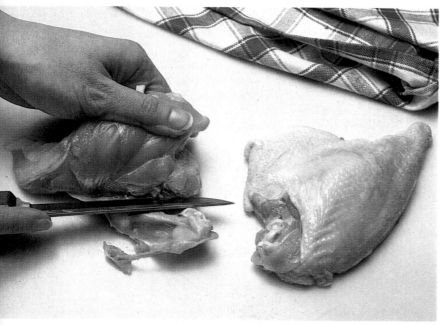

Step 4—Using the bone as a guide for the knife, continue separating the meat from the bone and rib cage. The chicken breast half is now deboned. Repeat procedure with remaining breast half.

Step 5—For a flatter chicken breast, locate the natural separation of the breast where the bone was removed. Lift

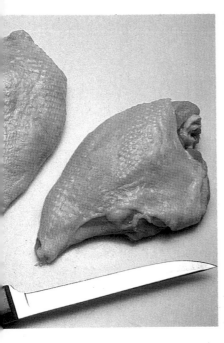

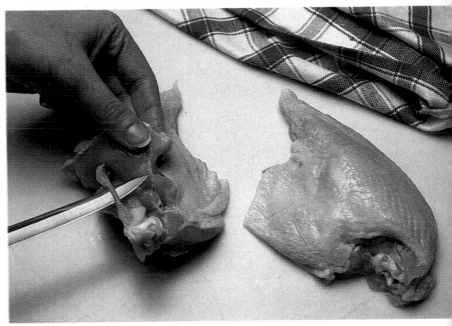

*Step 3—Locate the exposed joint at the meatiest
end of the breast; place cutting edge of
knife toward the bone. Separate the meat
from the bone, guiding the knife along the length
of the bone, continuing around the tip
of the bone and up the underside to the joint.*

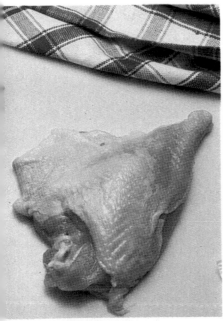

*the top layer, and using the
top of the knife, cut through the
thin membrane along the length
of the chicken breast half.*

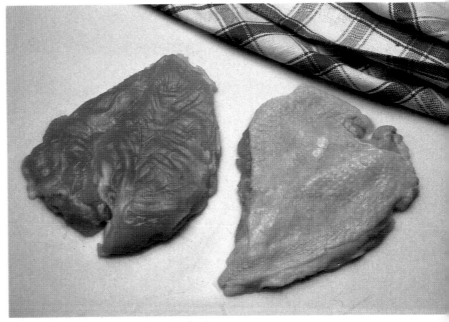

*Step 6—Unfold the chicken breast into a
triangular shape. Proceed with recipe as directed.*

TRUSSING A BIRD

Step 1—Place bird on back, and lightly stuff craw with dressing. Pull neck skin up and over stuffing.

Step 2—Secure neck skin to back of bird with a skewer. Lift wingtips up and over back, tucking under bird securely.

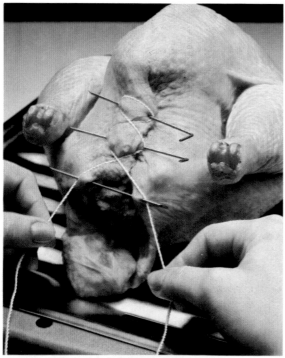

Step 3—Place bird, breast side up, on rack; lightly stuff dressing into cavity. Close with skewers and lace.

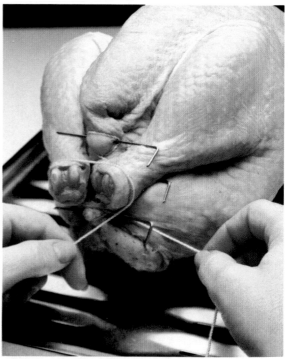

Step 4—Wrap ends of lacing around ends of legs. Pull string or cord down and wrap around tail, securing tightly.

FRYING A CHICKEN

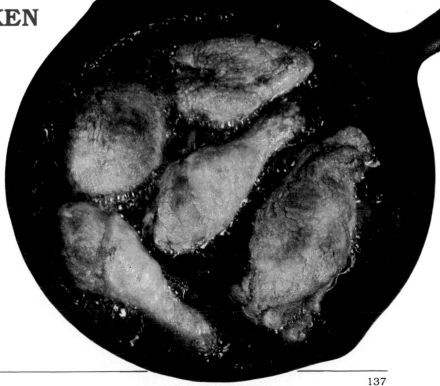

Step 1—After soaking chicken in salted water, lightly towel dry the pieces. Coat with seasoned flour. Dip into beaten egg (sometimes mixed with a little water) or buttermilk. Coat again with flour or fine crumbs. Let the pieces dry on a rack for half an hour before frying.

Step 2—Add coated chicken pieces to cooking oil or shortening which is hot enough to start browning chicken immediately. Space pieces apart to allow oil to bubble around all sides. When pieces are browned, reduce heat. Continue cooking until meat is fork tender.

ACKNOWLEDGMENTS

Recipe Credits

A Brown Fricassee, A White Fricassee, Chicken with Oyster Sauce, Curried Chicken, Maryland Chicken Pudding, Maryland Chicken Salad, Maryland Fried Chicken with Cream Gravy, Roast Ducklings with Cornbread Stuffing, Roast Goose with Potato and Peanut Stuffing, Southern Fried Chicken, Stewed Chicken with Light Dumplings adapted from *Maryland's Way* by Mrs. Lewis R. Andrews and Mrs. J. Reaney Kelly. By permission of The Hammond-Harwood House Association, Annapolis, Maryland, ©1966.

Alabama Chicken Spaghetti, Crusty Buttermilk Fried Chicken, Pickled Green Beans adapted from *Huntsville Heritage Cookbook*. Published by the Junior League of Huntsville, Alabama. By permission of the Junior League of Huntsville.

Baked Chicken in Scuppernong Wine, Charleston Chicken Pilaf, Coastal Fried Chicken with Brown Crumb Gravy, Onion Dressing Patties, Paella Valenciana, Potato Stuffing adapted from *The Southern Cook Book* by Marion Brown. By permission of University of North Carolina Press, Chapel Hill, North Carolina, ©1951.

Basic Baked Chicken, Basic Barbecued Chicken, Chicken Mousse, Chicken Piccata, Colonial Roast Chicken with Celery Stuffing, Country-Fried Chicken, Easy Chicken Gumbo, Eliza Pinckney's Chicken Fricassee, Festive Roast Chicken with Tennessee Country Sausage Stuffing, Fried Chicken with Saw Mill Gravy, Giblet Gravy, Marinated Grilled Chicken, South Carolina Barbecued Chicken, Spit Roasted Cornish Hens with Raisin Pecan Stuffing adapted from collection of the National Broiler Council.

Basic Roast Turkey courtesy of National Turkey Federation.

Batter Fried Chicken, Roast Chicken with Shrimp Stuffing, Roast Turkey with Sausage-Cornbread Stuffing adapted from *Aunt Hank's Rock House Kitchen*, compiled by Georgia Mae Smith Ericson. By permission of Crosby County Pioneer Memorial Museum, Crosbyton, Texas, ©1977.

Bread Dressing, Country Captain, Mary Randolph's Chicken Pudding, Old Dominion Fried Chicken with Gravy, Rosy Ducklings, Turkey-Sausage Casserole, Virginia Smothered Chicken adapted from *Virginia Cookery, Past and Present* by The Women's Auxiliary of Olivet Episcopal Church, Franconia, Virginia, ©1957. By permission of The Women's Auxiliary of Olivet Episcopal Church, Franconia.

Broiled Tomatoes, Chicken Coliseum, Ham and Chicken Jambalaya, Oyster Soup à la New Orleans, Poached Pears Julianne, Stew-Hole Chicken Fricassee adapted from the collection of the Hermann-Grima Historic House, New Orleans, Louisiana. By permission of the Hermann-Grima Historic House.

Brunswick Stew, Chicken with Sweet Potato Crust, Dixie Chicken Shortcake adapted from *50 States*, compiled by Culinary Arts Institute, ©1977. By permission of The Culinary Institute of America, Hyde Park, New York.

Buttery Fried Chicken adapted from *The Gasparilla Cookbook* by The Junior League of Tampa, Florida, ©1961. Courtesy of Mrs. Katherine Morgan.

Cajun menu, page 6, prepared for photography at Chez Marcelle Restaurant, Lafayette, Louisiana.

Carolina Apple Pie adapted from *North Carolina and Old Salem Cookery* by Elizabeth Hedgecock Sparks, ©1955. By permission of Elizabeth Hedgecock Sparks.

Carolina Chicken and Drop Dumplings adapted from *South Carolina Cookbook* by the South Carolina Homemakers Council, ©1953. By permission of The University of South Carolina Press, Columbia, South Carolina.

Cavatoni Chicken Eggplant Francesca adapted from *Feasting in New Orleans* by Joy Love Murray. By permission of Moran Publishing Co., New Orleans, Louisiana, ©1979.

Chef Crawford's Breast of Turkey Supreme courtesy of Chef Fred Crawford, Williamsburg, Virginia.

Chess Pie, Egg Custard Pie courtesy of Mrs. Helen Felder, Summitt, Mississippi.

Chicken à la King adapted from *Harris County Heritage Society Cook Book*. Published by The Harris County Heritage Society, Houston, Texas, ©1964. By permission of the Harris County Heritage Society.

Chicken à la Marengo, Thomas Jefferson's Fricassee, White Wine Fricassee adapted from *Thomas Jefferson's Cookbook* by Marie Kimball. By permission of University Press of Virginia, Charlottesville, Virginia, ©1979.

Chicken and Drop Dumplings, Texas-Style, Chicken Wiggle, Paper Sack Chicken Barbecue, Ring Around Chicken, Texas-Style Fried Chicken, Turkey Spoonbread adapted from *Favorite Recipes of Texas*. Reprinted by Favorite Recipes Press, Nashville, Tennessee, ©1965. By permission of Favorite Recipes Press.

Chicken and Yellow Rice, Garlic Fried Chicken, Hopkins County Stew, Roast Ducklings Bigarade adapted from *A Taste of Texas*, edited by Jane Trahey. By permission of Random House, Inc., New York, ©1949.

Chicken Divan, Georgia Chicken Scallop, Oven-Fried Pecan Chicken, Buttermilk Fried Chicken adapted from *Grace Hartley's Southern Cookbook* by Grace Hartley. These recipes first appeared in the *Atlanta Journal*. By permission of Doubleday & Co., Inc., ©1976.

Chicken Fiesta adapted from *The Receiving Line Was 11 Years Long* by Mary Margaret Davis. By permission of Guynes Printing Company, El Paso, Texas, ©1975.

Chicken Hash, Party Chicken Spaghetti adapted from *Georgia Heritage* by The National Society of The Colonial Dames of America in the State of Georgia, Savannah, Georgia. By permission of The Colonial Dames of America in the State of Georgia, ©1979.

Chicken in a Shell, Roast Ducklings Supreme, Roast Squab Pilau, Turkey Hash adapted from *Famous American Recipes* by John and Marie Roberson. By permission of Marie Roberson Hamm, ©1957.

Chicken Livers Financière adapted from *The Plantation Cookbook* by The Junior League of New Orleans. By permission of Doubleday & Company, ©1972.

Chicken Marengo adapted from *The Farmington Cookbook*. Published by Farmington Historic Homes Foundation, ©1979. By permission of Historic Homes Foundation, Inc.

Chicken Mole courtesy of Mrs. Sandra Kondora, Harrison, Arkansas.

Chicken Omelet, Plantation Chicken Casserole, Virginia Creamed Chicken adapted from *Recipes from Old Virginia* by The Virginia Federation of Home Demonstration Clubs, ©1946. By permission of the Virginia Extension Homemakers Council.

Chicken Paprika, Chicken Sauté Mexicaine, 1948 Original Barbecue Sauce adapted from the collection of McIlhenny Company, Avery Island, Louisiana. By permission of McIlhenny Company.

Chicken Salad in Patty Shells, Edwards House Chicken, Symphony Chicken Loaf, Turkey au Rochambeau adapted from *The Jackson Cookbook*, compiled by Symphony League of Jackson, Mississippi, ©1971. By permission of Symphony League of Jackson.

Creole Fried Duckling adapted from *The Secret of Creole Cooking* by B.F. Trappey's Sons, Inc., ©1976. By permission of B.F. Trappey's Sons, Inc.

Crispy Fried Squab courtesy of Mrs. Clint Wyrick, Garland, Texas.

Deep-Fat Fried Chicken, Fried Rock Cornish Hens, Lemon Barbecued Turkey, Oven-Fried Chicken adapted from *All-Time Favorites* compiled by Marshall Miller and Frances Reasonover, Texas Agricultural Extension Service, The Texas A&M University System, College Station, Texas. By permission of Agricultural Communications Department.

Dirty Rice, Sauerkraut Stuffing, Texas-Style Fried Chicken adapted from *The Saga of Texas Cookery* by Sarah Morgan. By permission of The Texian Press, Waco, Texas, ©1981.

Duck Gumbo adapted from *From Texas Kitchens* by James Stroman. By permission of Gulf Publishing Co., Houston, Texas, ©1982.

Ducklings à la Carte, Pigeon Pie adapted from *Junior League of Dallas Cook Book*, ©1948. By permission of The Junior League of Dallas, Texas.

Escalloped Chicken, Georgia-Style adapted from *Frances Virginia Tearoom Cookbook* by Mildred Huff Coleman. By permission of Peachtree Publishers Limited, Atlanta, ©1982.

Garlic Roasted Ducklings, Kentucky Burgoo, Oven Barbecued Turkey adapted from *Out of Kentucky Kitchens* by Marion Flexner. By permission of Franklin Watts, Inc., New York, ©1981.

Golden Chicken Nuggets, Smoked Turkey adapted from *The Bush Family Cookbook*, courtesy of Mrs. Bob Morris, Dallas, Texas.

Grandmother's Chicken Pie adapted from *Guten Appetit!*, compiled by the Sophienburg Memorial Association, Inc., New Braunfels, Texas, ©1978. By permission of Sophienburg Museum.

Herbed Oven-Fried Chicken adapted from *Woodlawn Plantation Cookbook*, courtesy of Woodlawn Plantation Council, National Trust for Historic Preservation, Mt. Vernon, Virginia.

Hermann-Grima Hospitality menu, page 90, prepared for photography at the Hermann-Grima House, New Orleans, Louisiana.

Highland Park Chicken Salad Sandwiches courtesy of Highland Park Pharmacy, Dallas, Texas, Mr. T. Bolan, Owner.

Mother's Chicken Spaghetti, Peach Cobbler adapted from *Southern Sideboards* by the Junior League of Jackson, Mississippi, ©1978. By permission of the Junior League of Jackson.

Oyster-Stuffed Breast of Chicken adapted from *Winston-Salem's Heritage of Hospitality* by the Junior League of Winston-Salem, North Carolina. By permission of the Junior League of Winston-Salem, ©1975.

Peanut Dressing adapted from *Two Hundred Years of Charleston Cooking*, edited by Lettie Gay, ©1976. By permission of The University of South Carolina Press, Columbia, South Carolina.

Pot-Roasted Chicken adapted from *James K. Polk Cookbook*, compiled by the James K. Polk Memorial Auxiliary, Columbia, Tennessee, ©1978. By permission of the James K. Polk Memorial Auxiliary.

Savannah Fried Chicken adapted from *The Savannah Sampler*. By permission of The Donning Company Publishers, Norfolk, Virginia, ©1978.

Sherried Cornish Hens adapted from *The Gasparilla Cookbook* by The Junior League of Tampa, Florida, ©1961. Courtesy of Mrs. W.E. Sumner.

The Duke of Windsor Sandwich adapted from *Neiman-Marcus — A Taste of the Past*, Neiman-Marcus, Dallas, Texas. By permission of Neiman-Marcus.

The Homestead Fried Chicken adapted from collection of The Homestead, Hot Springs, Virginia. Courtesy of The Homestead

Turkey Soufflé adapted from *The Gasparilla Cookbook* by the Junior League of Tampa, Florida, ©1961. Courtesy of Mrs. Jack Silbur.

Virginia Roast Duckling adapted from collection of Mrs. J.M. Barnhardt, Sr., Urbanna, Virginia. By permission of Mr. J.M. Barnhardt, Jr.

Wild Rice Dressing adapted from *Pioneer Kitchen*, published by Conklin Litho of San Diego, California. ©1971 by Ethel Reed. By permission of Conklin Litho.

INDEX
